The Masterpiece

Your College Journey as a Work of Art

By Ronald D. Dillard, Ph.D.

With a Foreword by Dr. Nhung N. Tran-Davies

Illustrations by Jessica Kroes Cooper

Copyright © 2025 by Ronald D. Dillard

All rights reserved.

No portion of this book may be reproduced in any form without written permission from the publisher or author, except as permitted by U.S. copyright law.

Book Cover by Clifton Jamaal Perry

Illustrations by Jessica Kroes Cooper

Edited by Julie Rickert

First edition 2025

This book is dedicated to the memory of Daziah Crawford, Vivian Battle, Iola Dillard, and Arthur "Robert" Dillard.

I also hope this is wind to the sails of Jonathan, Kristiana, and a host of nieces and nephews. Live life to the fullest.

Contents

Foreword 1

Introduction 3

1. Who Do You Want to Be? 5
2. Paying the Price of Admission 21
3. The Pitfalls of College 33

The Gallery 51

    ♦ Tanner Bosma 57

    ♦ Liz Burns 65

    ♦ Ronald Dillard, Ph.D. 75

    ♦ Monique Grayson 85

    ♦ Johnson Simon 93

    ♦ Nhung Tran-Davies 101

    ♦ Sruda Xedagbui 109

Acknowledgments

This book would not be possible without the synergy that came from the labor of several people. I want to thank the following individuals for their contributions to "The Masterpiece":

Tanner Bosma

Liz Burns

Kendra Dillard

Sheila Dillard

Steven Dillard

June Gothberg

Monique Grayson

Jessica Kroes-Cooper

Julie Rickert

Patrick Peoples

Clifton Jamaal Perry

Selena Roberts

Johnson Simon

Nhung Tran-Davies

Sruda Xedagbui

Foreword

Little did I know—when I was a four-year-old Vietnamese refugee girl, sitting in my mom's embrace, being tossed about in a small wooden fishing boat by the angry South China sea—that one day, I would become a physician and author, and that my journey would take me to Western Michigan University, where I would meet Dr. Ronald Dillard.

That encounter with Dr. Dillard and the Foundation Scholars he was working with was one of my most exhilarating experiences for how inspiring and transformative it was. I was invited to WMU to speak on the Resilience Factor but seeing how Dr. Dillard dedicated his life to lifting up a myriad of underprivileged students of varying backgrounds was truly awe-inspiring. These students who would not have otherwise succeeded in college or in life, because of the mountainous barriers facing them, were flourishing and reaching their dreams, not only from their own resilience, but in large part from Dr. Dillard's relentless support and guidance.

"The Masterpiece," therefore, has extra relevance and importance since Dr. Dillard has been in the trenches, first in his own life, then alongside his students. Coming from poverty and a single parent home, Dr. Dillard rose above the crime-ridden neighborhoods of Detroit because he learnt the value of education and how it can take him to exciting new places. His journey as an educator, in some of the most difficult circumstances, has shaped him into the down-to-earth, compassionate, and empathic man I met in Kalamazoo.

You hear his patient, gentle, nonjudgmental voice in "The Masterpiece" as he shares the lessons learnt. He knows the countless journeys many of his students have been on. He knows there is no one path to success. Through relatable anecdotes, Ron draws on his experiences to address the factors that go into deciding what we want to be to the many pitfalls that often break a student's dream. There is much wisdom, resourcefulness, and creativity in Dr. Dillard's guide to navigating the college journey.

As a physician, I have encountered all too often graduating high school students who are just lost. They have no idea how to even decide what they want to do for the rest of their life. Then, there are those post-secondary students who seem to be so bright and have so much potential yet are struggling to reach their dreams because of the pitfalls they've fallen into. I see the health consequences that arise from these struggles. As a former refugee, I am much saddened by the injustices that stem from students not attaining a full education, as I've learnt that "people can take everything away from you, but they can't take away your education."

This is why Dr. Dillard's book excites me so. It is because of my own education journey that led me to WMU where our paths crossed. Dr Dillard's passion to see students beat the odds, reach their fullest potential, and achieve their dreams is truly inspiring and transformative. Students reading "The Masterpiece" will no longer feel defeated. They will come to realize that their college journey is a work of art, and they themselves hold the paint brush. And, most of all, they will also come to recognize their innate gifts and understand that they themselves are works of art—imperfect, yet masterpieces in their own way!

Dr. Nhung N. Tran-Davies

Introduction

The Mona Lisa has been deemed to be one of the most valuable works of art in the world. Valued at about 800 million dollars, the painting sits on permanent display at the Louvre Museum in Paris. Except for it being stolen and missing for two years, the painting has been on display since 1797. The woman in the painting is somewhat of a mystery as historians have debated who the person could be. Some say it is the wife of a famous Italian businessman, but there hasn't been concrete proof to her real identity. In fact, historians haven't been able to determine when the painting was actually done, though most agree it was in the 1500s. And though this oil painting has been admired by many people around the world, it isn't nearly as valuable as you are. You, like the Mona Lisa, are a work of art. Yet, your beauty and potential are still in the works. You have your own paintbrush in your hands. You can craft your life artistically through education and the legacy you leave through your works. You may feel like you don't know exactly what those accomplishments will be. That's OK, because developing works of art (and futures) takes time, planning, effort, and collaboration. This book was written with your future in mind. It is meant to help you to think about your future and realize your dreams through education. So, roll up your sleeves, grab your paintbrush, and begin painting. Perhaps centuries from now folks will come from all around to admire your works the way they have admired Leonardo da Vinci's Mona Lisa.

Every work of art begins with an idea. Before a great piece is painted or sculpted, the artist envisions what he or she wishes to do with their medium. The goal may be to paint a landscape or uncover a face from stone using a chisel. However, that goal cannot be achieved without a vision. The same can be said about your future. Regardless of what you wish to do with your life, hard work and dedication are needed for it to become a true masterpiece. This does not mean that you will not make mistakes. In fact, some of the most popular art pieces in the world have flaws. For example, the popular sculpture called "David" by Michelangelo is flawed. The man carved from the marble stone is not anatomically correct because he is missing a muscle in his back. And though the artist could not correct the anatomy of his model due to a flaw in the marble, many still consider the carving a masterpiece. The lesson we can take from David is that one does not have to be perfect to be a work of art.

I would argue that imperfections and mistakes provide the best opportunities to learn. It is often told that Michael Jordan, arguably the best basketball player ever, did not make his high school basketball team when he first tried out. However, the young athlete didn't retreat into oblivion. Instead, MJ honed his skills, making sure that he would outwork and outlast any person, team, or coach who doubted his abilities. The rest, as they say, is history. Like Air Jordan himself, you can hone your skills and use your gifts to create your own work of art. Your journey will not be free from blemish, but with some knowledge and effort, you can be a legend in your own way.

I have met some amazing individuals during my journey as a student and educator. Some of those people have been gracious enough to share their stories with me and I present them in the following pages. It is my hope that you can learn from their stories and empower yourself to thrive on your own.

I'm rooting for you!

Sincerely,
Ronald D. Dillard, Ph.D.

Chapter 1

Who Do You Want to Be?

"Education is the passport to the future, for tomorrow belongs to those who prepare for it today." – Malcolm X

In this chapter, you will be able to:

    A. Begin to think about what your major could be.
    B. Explore various industries and fields of study.
    C. Assess yourself to see what careers better fit you.

Adults often ask children, "What do you want to be when you grow up?" It's a question that gets kids to think about their future. When little Johnny says, "I want to be a police officer or a firefighter" it may be because of what he has seen on television or inspired by his most recent Halloween costume. The intent of the question is excellent; however, the execution often misses the mark. The inquiry should go a lot deeper than that. The question is shortsighted because it is lacking the depth necessary to complete the vision for a life well-lived. Most of us would be miserable if we allowed our six-year-old selves to decide what we should do with the rest of our lives.

It's true that unless you know where you're going, it is nearly impossible to navigate the way there. For example, if you tell your GPS to take you to get pizza, it may lead you to a local pizzeria or to one in Albuquerque. This is fine if you have unlimited time and resources at your disposal to get food. However, if you're like most of us, you need to be more specific in your pursuit of your palatable pie. The same is true with selecting a future career. It is fine for children to think of careers they would like to pursue later in life. However, it's more crucial that they have a route, guidance, and a specific destination.

In order for students to select a career, they must first be exposed to a wide array of potential careers from which to choose. Sticking with the pizza analogy, you must consider that pizza is a choice from a wide array of foods. There are other options that you could choose from (hamburger, salad, pasta, etc.). Chances are that a person choosing pizza for dinner has had it before, or at bare minimum are aware that it is an option. Similarly, a child may express interest in becoming a police officer or firefighter because they have had exposure to those careers through their toys and television shows they watch. Yet, there are many more options that young people can explore. When was the last time you heard a young person say they wanted to be an audiologist? An orthoptist? A physician's assistant? A logistician?

Most likely, the answer is you haven't heard a student (or yourself) mention these careers. I challenge you to look these (and other careers) up. The more you know, the more likely you will be able to select a career that fits you, your talents, skills, and preferences.

E.S.P.

Did you know that "ESP" traditionally means Extra Sensory Perception? This refers to a person's ability to perceive things that we can't see, taste, touch, hear, or smell. Some people call it a sixth sense. You may have seen this portrayed in a movie where a character can read the minds of others, "see" the future, or communicate with ghosts. Many people do not believe that having a sixth sense is possible, but in this book, ESP means "Exposure, Skills, and Passion." And they are very real!

Manufacturers have learned something from studying consumer habits. They know that if they offer consumers more options, they will sell more products. When you go into a store for shoes, you will notice that shoes come in many colors, shapes, and sizes. They are hoping that you will find something that fits your needs and tastes and leave after making a purchase. The same can be done with shopping for a career. Instead of going to the mall, however, you will find what you need by searching the web, visiting your local library, and networking with a diverse group of friends and associates. Similar to shopping for shoes, you are looking for a perfect fit for you. To do this, you will need to expose yourself to careers, analyze the skills you have developed (in school and outside), and follow your passion. I like to call this process using your ESP.

Exposure

A great way to shop for a career is to have exposure to the people and careers around you. Most people work in one industry or another. As you go about your day, try to count the different careers you see represented. Most likely, you will see teachers (education), police officers (law enforcement), store managers (retail), bank tellers (finance), and others. On other days, you may encounter your doctor (health care), a plumber (skilled trade), a chef (food service), or an insurance agent (insurance). I encourage you to ask the people you encounter about their work and education. You will find that most of them will be friendly and inviting. People tend to enjoy talking about their successes and helping curious others to succeed.

The purpose of these conversations is to allow you to gain exposure to a given career to decide if you should take a closer look. Similar to window shopping at the mall, you may be intrigued enough to go in and try them on (the career, that is). However, if you decide after your inquiry that working in insurance, for example, is not a good "fit" for you, you can continue shopping for something "in your size."

Not every request you make of professionals will be granted. Some people will be very busy and some may not be interested in helping you on your journey. That's ok! When you run into this type of resistance, just keep moving along. I have tried on shoes in my size that looked nice on the shelf. However, they didn't look or feel right on my feet. That didn't stop me from wearing shoes! The benefit of moving on to your next person will pay off for you in the long run. Remember, this is about you, not them.

Once you have found a supportive person in a career that interests you, you have struck gold! Through this relationship, you can observe the person as they do their work and ask them questions you may be reluctant to ask a stranger. For example, it may be considered impolite to ask a total stranger about the "behind the scenes" factors of their job. This may include information on the actual hours they work in a week, their least favorite parts of the work, and salary. However, once you have established a relationship with a working professional, they may feel free to share with you all of the juicy details.

Remember, though, that you must ESTABLISH a relationship first. Ask the person what topics are off limits if you're unsure. And like all great relationships, spend time getting to know the person. You probably don't want to ask them how much money they make during your first encounter. Hopefully, however, you can build upon your interactions and even exchange phone numbers. Remember, though, you want to ask permission first. If they are willing to exchange numbers, you can likely text them to stay connected, but establish rules. Your professional pal may not want you to text them after 6 PM (or some other restriction). It's important that you respect their personal time and space. After all, they are helping you a great deal and if you come on too strong, you may sour the relationship before it begins to pay off.

> Some questions for you to consider asking professionals:
> - What did you study in college?
> - What have you learned in your career that you wished you knew long ago?
> - How do you manage stress at work?
> - What skills should I work on outside of school to be successful in this career?
> - Are there trends in the industry that I should know about?
> - How much money should I expect to earn in my first job?

Let your supportive person know that you are searching for a career path that fits your needs. This is important so they will understand that you are not committing yourself to their chosen field, but simply doing your research. You may find that they will introduce you to other supportive people in other industries. This will help you to gain exposure to even more information, and at this point, you need all the information you can get. You will be amazed at the seeds that this information will plant in your mind and the fruit that will come from these seeds later in life.

For example, as a high school student, I had a supportive adult by the name of Mark. Mark was an auto mechanic and as a result, he had a very busy schedule. In addition to working on cars, Mark had a family to support. He would always say, "Time isn't money; I can always make money, but I can never make more time." This statement was in reference to his desire to spend more time with family and friends.

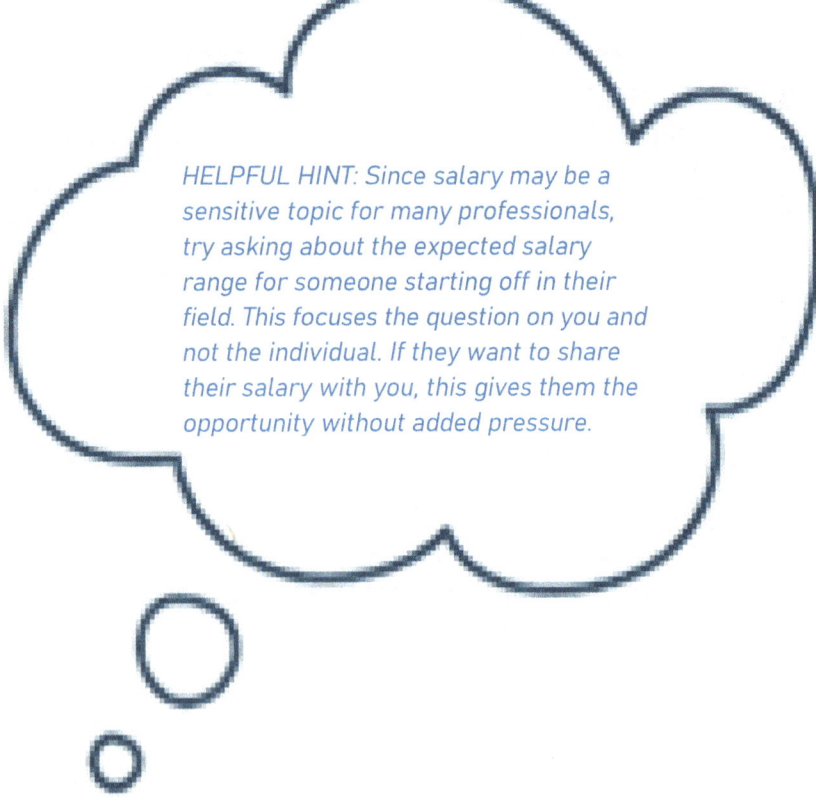

HELPFUL HINT: Since salary may be a sensitive topic for many professionals, try asking about the expected salary range for someone starting off in their field. This focuses the question on you and not the individual. If they want to share their salary with you, this gives them the opportunity without added pressure.

Mark planted a seed in my mind that sticks with me to this day. He taught me to prioritize the things in my life and have a healthy balance between work and other things that matter in life. Even though I did not go into the business of working on cars, this lesson serves to keep my life revving in the right direction.

You may be wondering, "How much exposure should I get?" Well, there really isn't one correct answer. One should get as much exposure as one needs to make an informed decision about careers. In this case, it is less important to ascribe a specific number of jobs or industries. A more important question is, "Have I found something that really interests me?" If you haven't, then you should keep getting more and more exposure. Later on, we will discuss PASSION, which is an equally important factor to consider. Exposure to various careers is vital because you may discover that your passion aligns with a career that is new to you. In this way, Exposure begins opening doors that were closed to you before. In addition, browsing industries and careers may reveal new passions to you. Think of it this way: what if Serena Williams was never exposed to tennis or Dr. Mae Jemison never exposed to science?

For those of you who are looking for a mathematical formula to using exposure, consider the power of three! In other words, select three industries and three careers in each one. For example, Valerie is a ninth-grade student from Michigan. She is interested in becoming a teacher. However, her father is an attorney and believes that Valerie should pursue a career in law. Valerie's mother owns a bakery and encourages her to pursue whatever makes her happy, although she would love it if Valerie would follow in her footsteps as an entrepreneur.

My recommendation would be for Valerie to explore all three industries listed above: education, law, and food service. For each industry, I would encourage Valerie to research 3 career paths, as shown in this chart:

Industry	Career option 1	Career option 2	Career option 3
Education	Kindergarten Teacher	School Counselor	High School Teacher
Law	Attorney	Paralegal	FBI Agent
Food Service	Chef	Health Inspector	Entrepreneur

If Valerie does her homework on these careers, she may find that her father's recommendation is or isn't the right fit for her. She may discover that there are areas of overlap within these fields. For example, she could work to become a law professor, which would combine education and law. The most important aspect of exposure is that one finds and prepares for a career that will be the vehicle to take them where they want to go in life.

Gaining exposure is work. Just as the shoes at the mall aren't going to come to you, you must take the time and put forth the effort to search out a field that fits you and your lifestyle. More importantly, your career will stick with you longer than a pair of shoes. Yet, if you do your research early (I suggest as early as 6th grade), you will not be burdened with this work while you are a student in college. Just as an Olympian prepares for the gold medal well in advance of the event, so does the well-prepared college student.

Skills

All humans have innate gifts they are born with, but skills require development. These gifts, for the sake of this conversation, are like the raw materials used to make something greater. For example, the carbon required to make a diamond is black and dull like charcoal. However, it takes time, heat, tremendous pressure, and a trained gemologist to transform that material into the glittering stones many of us use to adorn ourselves. Your natural gifts, like the carbon, must be developed and transformed into something spectacular.

Watching Serena Williams play tennis is a treat. She owns the court. No matter where the ball bounces, she has developed an uncanny ability to get there and send it careening over the net, out of her opponent's reach. She is likely the most accomplished tennis player to ever play the game. Some say that she is the greatest athlete ever. While this may be up for debate, what isn't debatable is the fact that she was not born with the skills she has today. Being a skilled tennis player is something that she has worked to develop. Sure, she was likely born with physical and mental gifts that have allowed her to become so dominant, but strengthening muscles, gaining speed, and athletic intelligence have come through hours upon hours of hard work.

In the case of Serena Williams, it probably helps that she is 5'9" tall, but without hard work and dedication, her skills would not be what they are today. Serena's height is a natural gift, but her speed on the court is a skill that she has honed. Her height alone is not enough to earn all of the accolades that she has. Otherwise, every woman standing 5'9" tall would be as dominant.

As a child, I remember watching Venus and Serena Williams as their stars began to rise. At that time, they were children themselves. Still growing and underdeveloped, they wore beads in their hair as they traversed the awkward stage of adolescence. Those beads and their father's relentless approach to the game were the two constants I remember about them. These two young ladies honed their skills in Compton, California, before moving on to other places to perfect their game. Around that time in life, I was tinkering around with a trumpet that my mother bought me to join a school band. The difference between my trumpet playing and the Williams sisters' tennis playing is that they continued to play and get better. When playing the trumpet became too burdensome to me, I gave it up. As a result, my skill set with the trumpet is not something folks would pay to hear.

I wonder what kind of musician I would be today if I had persisted, practiced, and perfected that craft. I suppose I'll never know. That's how the cookie crumbles sometimes. Better yet, that's how the ball bounces.

A skill is an ability to do something well. Skills can be rooted in the natural gifts that you possess as a human being or be an adaptation you make in order to reach a goal. For example, a former student of mine named Sam has an uncanny ability to play the piano by ear. If he hears a song once, he can play it back. However, Sam would like to attend Juilliard and study music theory. In order to do that, Sam must learn to read and compose music. Therefore, his natural musical talent must be enhanced by learning this skill. His gift for music requires him to work to develop a skill needed to get the education he desires.

As mentioned before, all human beings are born with gifts. Some people are athletically gifted with good genes to grow to be tall or have an unusual wingspan. Others of us have creative minds that allow us to excel in music or other arts. Still, others of us are blessed to be able to connect with people exceptionally well. Have you ever seen a person that can walk into a room and mingle with strangers with ease? They can leave any social situation making friends with folks who were strangers 20 minutes earlier.

These innate gifts are truly incredible and benefit those of us who recognize what we have. Examples of innate abilities appear vividly in nature. For example, sea turtles venture onto beaches to lay eggs, covering them in sand. When those eggs hatch, the baby turtles innately (without being taught) scurry to the ocean to begin their lives under the safety of the waves. If they're not hasty to get to the sea, they can be gobbled up by predators.

Like the sea turtle, you have innate gifts within you. If you know what they are, you can work to develop skills to complement those gifts. Observant parents, teachers, and friends may point these gifts out to you. You may also be watchful and notice these characteristics in yourself. What's most important is that you nurture them. Apparently, Richard Williams saw something in his daughters, nurtured their gifts, and developed them into a skill that has been unmatched in the world of tennis.

In addition to innate gifts, learn from your supportive people the skills that may not come naturally, but are necessary to acquire to reach your goal. These may be things in which you have no interest, but are vital for your career. For example, it is widely known that many people have a fear of public speaking. When faced with the idea of delivering a speech to an audience, some folks freeze up or avoid the situation altogether. Yet, public speaking is a skill that is necessary for success in many careers.

If you want to be a lawyer, a teacher, or a doctor, you will need to develop the skill of public speaking. Many folks in these professions use the skill of speaking to an audience as a regular function of their jobs. Lawyers speak in court. Teachers present information in the classroom. Doctors often deliver information to their peers and patients in this format. Yet, speaking is not just relegated to these settings. In many cases, public speaking will be a part of the interview process to get the job you want.

More and more employers are asking job candidates to give presentations during the process of interviewing. They are checking to see if you would be a good representative of their organization. Therefore, public speaking—whether it may be a fear that you have or not—should be a skill that you begin cultivating now. Odds are you will have to be comfortable enough with that skill to get the job you want and advance in the career.

Innate abilities	Skills
20/20 Vision	Piloting a plane
Height/Wingspan	Basketball agility
Multi-octave vocal range	Singing on key
Steady hands	Performing surgery

Passion

According to the dictionary, passion is "an almost uncontrollable emotion." Passion is a part of the human experience because we all feel emotions. Many times, these emotions are highlighted in the movies we watch and the songs we sing growing up. For example, most of us are familiar with the song that commands us to clap our hands if we're happy and we know it. The song takes the feeling of happiness and gives us a way to express it with our family and friends. Indeed, this is exactly how passion should be channeled. If there is a persistently present emotion that we have, we should direct that passion into the work that we do. A famous quote by Mark Twain says, "Find a job you enjoy doing and you'll never work a day in your life."

I believe Mark Twain meant that our jobs or careers can be taxing on us as humans when passion is missing. Simply getting out of bed to go to a job that one does not enjoy is a miserable task. On the other hand, waking up to go to a job that you're passionate about is a different story altogether. In other words, once you have exposed yourself to various industries and careers, it's important that you remember to consider your passions. Otherwise, your career will be more of a necessary burden than an enjoyable way to finance your life.

Just think about the people you have encountered on their jobs. It's apparent when someone is simply doing a job for a paycheck. It is evident in how they interact with others and the expression on their face. Most likely you have encountered an employee of an organization whose enthusiasm for their job is nonexistent. They may not have greeted you; they may not have looked you in the eye, and in some cases they may not have spoken to you at all. As a customer, you probably did not feel appreciated. In some cases, you may avoid the organization in the future.

In other cases, you may have gotten exceptional customer service. For example, there was a commercial for Wal-Mart that featured two gentlemen who worked as greeters in a Wal-Mart store. These gentlemen talked about how they did their job, happily, smiling, and going the extra mile to make customers feel welcome. They remembered their customers by name and even gave hugs to people who welcomed that sort of familiarity. It was evident to those who watched the commercial that these gentlemen had a passion for the work that they did. That passion allowed the greeters to do their job with enthusiasm and build relationships with customers. In turn, Wal-Mart retains customers who will shop in their stores for years to come.

If a passion for people can encourage people to be exceptional greeters for Wal-Mart, then your passion for (fill in the blank) can encourage you to be an exceptional (fill in the blank).

You may be wondering how you will know when you discover your passion. To answer that question, I'll ask you to consider two pieces of advice:

1. You may be passionate about more than one thing.

Example: I am passionate about working with youth. I am passionate about music.

2. Your passions—unlike a fad, a pastime, or a hobby—will last for a lifetime.

The Masterpiece

Example: I played the trumpet to pass time in high school. Playing that instrument was a pastime, but enjoying music as a listener and concertgoer is one of my passions. I am always ready to listen to music.

To drive these points home, I'll share with you a story about a student. For the purposes of this story, we'll call the student "Jane." Jane was a student that I met during my time as a teacher in a detention center. Jane was 15 years old and angry. Jane's anger was different from the expected angst students felt while being detained. Unlike many of the other students, Jane refused to engage in activities with other students. She just wanted to write. As a matter of fact, Jane's detention stemmed from a dispute she had in school with a teacher. The incident stemmed from the teacher getting in the way of Jane's writing. The teacher had asked Jane to put away her journal and take a math test. When Jane refused, the teacher attempted to pull the journal from Jane's grasp. This led to a wrestling match in which the teacher's glasses were broken and Jane was arrested.

Knowing this information, the teaching staff at the detention center crafted a plan to allow Jane to journal in all of her classes, including classes where writing was not the focus. This allowed Jane to complete all of her work in her classes, while also pursuing her passion to write! It appeared that her motivation to complete non-writing work was writing. So, she would quickly and thoroughly do her work so that she could get to her journaling.

A few years later, I ran into Jane on a college campus. She was happy to report that she was pursuing a degree in journalism and creative writing. She had already garnered some recognition for the work she had done with her university's newspaper.

In addition, Jane had published a book of her poetry. Her smile said it all. As a bonus, Jane thanked me for allowing her to do what she loved while she was in my classroom.

She said, "When I wrote, I wasn't locked up anymore." Now that same passion will fuel a career that will be liberating to her for the rest of her life.

The lesson that we can learn from Jane is that our passion should not be ignored. Instead, it should be nurtured. While there will be times on our journey that we must engage in work that may be less interesting to us than what we're passionate about, that work may be necessary to allow us to pursue our passion. Jane mentioned that she was taking business classes because she wanted to learn more about marketing her work and publishing.

Like Jane, none of us are exactly sure where life is taking us. However, having knowledge and skills is always helpful. Having a knowledge base in business may help Jane to become a successful author, editor, or publisher. Lacking knowledge would only hurt her in the long run.

My best advice is for you to use your ESP to select a path on which to travel. In times of frustration or despair, use your passion to fuel your forward movement. Working without passion is like a car without fuel. You won't go far on an empty tank.

Chapter 2

Paying the Price of Admission

Terms to know for this chapter

Term	Definition
Tuition	The cost to take classes at a school. This cost can vary depending on the school you choose or whether you're a resident of the state or not.
Fees	The cost for other services at your school that are not related to your tuition. Example: You may pay a fee to be enrolled or a fee to support your institution's library.
Textbooks	In college, students purchase their books for school. Each semester will likely require a different set of books. The prices can be minimal or very expensive depending on the courses. Example: John's books for his first semester in college totaled $314.98.
Housing (room)	College students need a place to live. They can choose to live in campus housing or off campus. If you're concerned about your budget, you may investigate what's the best option, including living at home with family.

Term	Definition
Food (board)	Food is a necessity for living. Many institutions offer meal plans for students to eat. However, if you don't live on campus, you may need to do your own shopping and meal preparation. Either way, there is a cost associated with eating.
Grant	Grants are free money. You don't have to pay it back. Consider it a gift. Sometimes grants are based on your income or other factors.
Scholarship	Scholarships are financial gifts that students usually apply to receive. There is almost always a deadline to apply and an academic requirement such as a GPA or level in school. Scholarships, like grants, do not have to be paid back. Instead, you "pay" for them with your academic performance.
Loans	Loan means you're borrowing money. You must pay them back with interest. In other words, you will pay more back than you actually received. You should only borrow money if you <u>need</u> it. Grants and scholarships are better because there is no obligation to pay them back.
FAFSA	This means "Free Application for Federal Student Aid." If you want to apply for federal grants and/or loans, you must fill this out. You will need to provide information about your income and your parents' income in most cases.

Term	Definition
Aid year	The FAFSA will make you eligible to receive funds for a specified period of time called the "aid year." The aid year begins on July 1st and goes to June 30th of the following year. If you're planning to go to college in the fall of 2025 or the winter/spring of 2026, you should fill out the FAFSA for the 2025-2026 aid year. An application must be filled out for every aid year you intend to receive financial aid.
SAI (formerly EFC)	A figure called the Student Aid Index (SAI) is the amount of money the federal government determines that your family can pay for your college expenses during the aid year. This is based on your family's income and net worth. Families that make more money generally have a higher SAI. Families with less income tend to have a lower SAI.
Major	This refers to a student's field of study. Institutions have put together requirements for students to complete in order to earn a degree. Some examples of majors include Education, Biology, Business, or Engineering. Simply put, your major is the field your studies prepare you to enter.

Buying a car can be a fun, exhilarating process. There are so many vehicles to choose from. You could get a convertible, a sedan, an SUV, a minivan, something new, something from Craigslist, or take a gently used vehicle from a family member. The possibilities seem endless when you consider all of the companies that manufacture vehicles, each offering different models with different features to entice a wide pool of buyers.

One factor that almost always plays into which car we choose (or whether we get a car at all) is price. Taking Aunt Bessie's 1998 Buick actually turns out to be a great deal if it is free. It definitely beats having to have a down payment and financing a vehicle with monthly payments. When you consider paying for insurance, gas, and maintenance, buying a car seems to be an investment that some high school and college students find hard to make.

Consider this! No one would buy a car and then test drive it. The test drive should happen before any money exchanges hands. A wise car shopper may even take the car they're interested in purchasing to a mechanic to get a professional opinion. This way, you won't be stuck with a lemon.

Paying for college can be even more complex than paying for your first set of wheels. Like cars, there are many different options that should be considered. Should you go to a 4-year university? Should you try community college first? Should you apply for scholarships or loans? Answering those questions first can make a big difference in how much you actually pay for college. And yet, you must remember to answer the most important question: What am I going to study? Hopefully, you have spent time and energy using your ESP (see Chapter 1) to determine your educational and career path. Selecting a school and major should be something that you have considered long before you arrive to your campus.

Doing your research on a car before you purchase it can save you some money and reduce stress. Doing your research on colleges can save you the same. However, you'll get more miles out of your education than your first car. As a matter of fact, once you have developed a financial plan for attending college, you may actually come to the realization that a car is not in your budget. Yet, don't panic. Having a well thought out financial plan for your education will pay off. When choosing vehicles, the best option is the one that travels on your "wills" not "wheels."

Cost of Attendance

As you are thinking about colleges, it's important to know how much your education will cost you. This is called "cost of attendance." In the cost of attendance, you can expect to see **tuition, fees, books, housing, food**, and other expenses. Most institutions will put these numbers together based on what it costs for the average student to attend. However, it is important that you keep in mind that there may be additional costs depending on your **major** or where you live. So, it's important to determine if the "cost of attendance" for your school of choice is the actual amount it will cost for you. College—like cars, shoes, and clothes—is not a "one size fits all" item. You may see this point proven in an advertisement for a car. Many times, the advertiser will show you the price for a base model; however, when you factor in the air conditioning, sound system, heated seats, and floor mats, the price jumps drastically. So, buyer be knowledgeable. Find out if the cost that your institution advertises includes all the bells and whistles you will need to be successful. There may be some fees that you are not expecting, so doing your research on your exact fit as a student will help you to avoid surprises down the road.

You will notice when you look at an institution's cost of attendance they will provide you an amount for **"in-state tuition"** and **"out-of-state tuition."** Students who have lived, and have residency, in the state they plan to attend college are charged in-state tuition. This amount is usually significantly less expensive than out-of-state tuition. Therefore, a student attending a Michigan college who grew up in Michigan and graduated from a high school in the state will pay less than a student who lived and graduated in Ohio. As a result, when you are pricing colleges, you may consider going to school in your home state. This could potentially save you a lot of money down the stretch. After all, many colleges receive funds from the state. The state gets its money from taxes paid by residents. So, technically, you're getting a break because you've already contributed to the institution's budget through state taxes.

Below are a few examples to demonstrate how tuition can differ for in-state students and out-of-state students.

Institution	In-state tuition*	Out-of-state tuition*
University of Michigan	$17,404	$60,614
Kansas State University	$10,242	$27,588
Ohio State University	$12,180	$26,778

*These costs were pulled from each institution's website in August 2024 for a freshman or sophomore student taking two semesters of 15 credit hours each. These numbers only represent tuition costs. They do not include room and board or other costs that go into "cost of attendance."

Another thing you will notice as you look at the cost of attendance for college is that prices vary. As with cars, there is a range in pricing that must be considered. Similarly, there are institutions that some consider to be the Mercedes-Benz of institutions, while others are more economical. This is why it is important that you have researched your colleges of interest. You may be able to get all the luxuries of a higher priced institution at a more reasonably priced school. When choosing a school, the name, sports record, and school traditions are not nearly as important as your own goals and ability to pay. It is especially important to consider that the number 1 reason students leave college is lack of funding. Which would you rather have: an incredible year at a big-name school, or a degree completed at a more affordable institution?

Private colleges, unlike public institutions, tend to be smaller and more expensive. So, if you're interested in attending a private college, you should expect to spend more money. These institutions do not receive government funding, so the bulk of their operations are funded from the tuition that their students pay. Additionally, there will likely be no cost difference for "in-state" and "out-of-state" students. For example, a student attending Kalamazoo College (a private college in Kalamazoo, Michigan) in the 2024-2025 aid year would pay $60,900 regardless of state residency. Yet, a student attending Western Michigan University (a public university that neighbors Kalamazoo College) would pay $15,126 (in-state student) or $18,908 (out-of-state student) for two semesters.

Another factor in how much you'll pay as a college student is what you'll study. Not all majors are created equal. Some majors come with fees that most other students do not pay. For example, a student studying Aviation may have fees associated with flying planes. Those fees include insurance, plane fuel, and instructor fees. Considering a pilot in training is required to practice flying for hundreds of hours before they can be certified to fly on their own, these fees can add several thousand dollars on top of the cost of attendance. Therefore, it is very important that students understand how much more they will pay if they choose a specialized program like aviation or some medical degrees. Similar to owning a car, you must consider the maintenance associated with your college journey. Maintaining a luxury vehicle is much more expensive than an economy vehicle, but they both get you to where you want to go.

Show Them the Money

Once you have been accepted to your school, you have to pay your bills shortly before classes begin. If you have the money saved to pay the cost of attendance, then you're very fortunate. However, if you are like most students, your financial plan will include grants, loans, or scholarships. Filling out the FAFSA

(Free Application for Federal Student Aid) could make you eligible for federal loans and some federal need-based grants. However, in general, grants and scholarships will have other requirements, such as family income and academic performance in high school or college admissions test scores for merit-based awards.

Scholarships are awarded to students who meet the requirements that the people who fund them have set forth. The requirements could be a certain GPA, test score, major, affiliation, or other attribute. The great news is that scholarships are plentiful. There will be some work in searching for scholarships, but the reward is well worth the effort. You can search online (www.fastweb.com seems to be popular) or in publications that can be found at the library or university. You may even find that your parents' employer may offer scholarships for children of employees. However, scholarships usually require some searching on your part. They typically do not come to find you. **My suggestion would be to search at least one hour per week until you have enough money to carry you through to graduation.**

Scholarships can range in monetary value so it's important that you understand how much money you will get if awarded. Still, most times, scholarships are stackable. In other words, you can get more than one and use them at once to pay for your schooling. However, you cannot enrich yourself personally from scholarships. For example, if your cost of attendance is $35,000, you can't receive a scholarship for $45,000 and pocket the $10,000 overage (in most cases). Keep in mind that many scholarships will require you to demonstrate that your education is a good investment, so keep your grades as high as possible. It's also important to know if your scholarship is a one-time gift or if it is renewable. Some funds can be an ongoing investment in your education as long as you continue to be eligible. If there is a grade requirement, these scholarships will continue to pay for future semesters if you keep up your end of the bargain by passing classes and keeping your grades respectable.

Grants, like scholarships, are gifts. Grants are sometimes based on "need," which means they will be given to students who demonstrate financial need. This is often determined by completing the FAFSA and having the federal government calculate your Student Aid Index (SAI, formerly known as the EFC). Simply put, families who have less income and assets will be eligible for more need-based funds. If you are from a family that is wealthy, it is highly unlikely that you will receive any need-based grants. However, there may be funds that your institution awards in the form of grants based on other factors. For example, a college may give a grant to students who want to study a certain field. If the institution wants to lure students to that field, grants may make that major attractive. For example, in states where there is a teacher shortage, grants may be available for students who want to be teachers. These grants may not have an academic requirement and they may be a one-time gift. So, be sure you understand how the funds fit into your big picture of funding. The grants could also have a stipulation attached that requires you to work in the state for a specified amount of time, so get a full understanding before you accept these gifts.

"Loans" is certainly a word that you've heard before. Perhaps it is even a word that you've used before. If a friend borrows $20 from you, you may agree to the loan with expectation that your friend will pay you back. Friends rarely expect more in return than they loaned out. However, the federal government and banks are different: they expect you to pay back what you borrowed, plus an additional amount called interest. There may also be fees associated with initiating the loan. So, when all is said and done, you will pay back the amount you borrowed plus fees and plus interest. Borrowing $1000 during a semester to purchase a computer may sound like a good idea; however, it is important that you understand that when it's time to pay up, you will pay back substantially more than $1000.

Interest rates vary; however, the interest that the government charges to students is typically better than borrowing from a bank. This is one area where you'll want to do some additional research. If you have shopped around for institutions, applied for scholarships and grants, and still are coming up short, you want to borrow as little money as possible. This way, you will have less to pay back. Student loans are incredibly easy to get and most times your school will make accessing the money simple by depositing the funds directly into your bank account. Yet, you shouldn't let ease of access lure you into a mound of debt that will take you the rest of your life to pay off. Remember, you have a lot of life ahead of you and you will want to keep the money you earn to live, invest, and play.

The last thing to discuss about loans is the type of loan you're getting from the government. The government will offer students either subsidized loans or unsubsidized loans. These two terms refer to interest that accrues while you're in school. As soon as you borrow money for the government or a bank, interest begins piling up like leaves on an autumn lawn. However, for subsidized loans, the government pays the interest while you're in school. So, in this case, it's like the government is raking up the leaves for you. This is a benefit which is based on family income. So, families who make more will receive less help from the government. Unsubsidized loans are the less desirable of the two types of loans. The government does not pay your interest, so the leaves are piling up. You can either pay the interest while you're in school, or let the interest pile up and add to the amount you will owe back later. Simply put, subsidized loans are better for you in the long run.

College is expensive, but paying for it does not have to be a mystery. Many college students pay dearly because they have not equipped themselves with the knowledge to make informed decisions. Think of it this way: when you are at a restaurant and you order a steak, you see the price on the menu. You should have an idea of how you will pay for that meal. You may have cash in your wallet, a credit card, or a gift card. If you pay for the meal with cash or a gift card, the transaction is done when you leave the table. However, if you paid using a credit card, you simply borrowed money from your credit card company, promising them you will pay for the meal and a little extra for the convenience of using the credit. My advice is that it's better to work hard beforehand to secure the funds (scholarships and grants) to walk away from college with no debt. However, if you do borrow, do so responsibly (as little loan as possible). Your older self will want to give your younger self a big hug, or perhaps a steak dinner. However, if you've managed your funding well, you may even be able to leave the waiter a cash tip.

Chapter 3

The Pitfalls of College

When I was a kid, video games were a lot less advanced than they are today. Atari 2600 was the hottest system in video game entertainment for the home. Today, however, you would find the graphics and sound an abomination to your eyes and ears. Back then, just playing the home version of Pac-Man brought joy to millions of gamers. Despite having primitive sound effects and horribly pixelated animation, kids were just happy to be playing their favorite arcade games on their floor model TV's (look up floor model TV for a laugh) (as a matter of fact look up Atari 2600 games for an even bigger laugh). These games today would not likely keep your attention for longer than 30 seconds. Without question, your smart phone is more powerful and more valuable than 100 Atari 2600 units.

My favorite game on Atari 2600 was 'Pitfall.' The game featured a jungle traversing gentleman named Pitfall Harry. Harry was reminiscent of another 80's movie character named Indiana Jones (yes, I recognize that you may have to look him up, too, but I'm making a point here). The protagonist of the 'Pitfall' games found himself running through the jungle trying to avoid all sorts of danger: alligators, scorpions, snakes, and of course the dreaded pitfalls (which sometimes housed hungry alligators). To get from one side of the pitfall to the other, the player had to swing from a vine like Tarzan. Your timing had to be just right to survive crossing the pit. If your timing was off and you fell to your doom, the game played a tune that echoed your own internal regret (seriously, look it up on YouTube).

In my experience working with college students, I have witnessed students falling into several pitfalls. No, they weren't devoured by gators, but often times their chances of graduating were greatly diminished, or at the very least postponed severely. Those pitfalls include lack of funding, poor time management, pregnancy, drugs (including alcohol), or lack of ESP (exposure, skills, and passion). If you are a student going to college or preparing to go to college and you do not have a plan, then college can ultimately be an expensive experiment. There are other, less expensive ways to explore than paying the cost of attendance at a college or university. If exploration is what you're looking for, you might enjoy dodging animals in the jungle on the worst video game platform you've ever witnessed in your lifetime. That would certainly be cheaper and less risky than aimlessly wandering through college on your own dime, or worse, loan money. However, if you want to avoid some of the pitfalls that can hinder your college graduation, continue reading on.

Pitfall 1: Insufficient Funds

The previous chapter is all about funding your college education. It details ways to pay for college without going into debt. However, I have worked with many college students who have not thought about funding at all. Believe it or not, some students enroll in college without having a financial plan or a clue how much college actually costs. I have had conversations with tearful students who owe thousands of dollars for their first semester of college and suddenly realize that they did not apply for any financial aid or scholarships. This pitfall is one of the largest for students enrolling in college because without a plan, college can easily gobble up your resources faster than a hungry gator.

Lacking a financial plan is one factor in this pitfall; poor spending habits is another. Once you have a financial plan to pay for college, you have to stick to it! Failing to do so is like preparing a Thanksgiving dinner and then ordering pizza instead of enjoying the feast at your table. Doing the work of planning financially is useless if you are going to abandon the plan. My recommendation is that your plan minimizes the use of loans and credit cards.

Once you're in college, you will instantly become a prime target for credit card companies. Getting one will be easier than getting a date. However, the interest will likely be more irritating than poison ivy (I'm sticking to this whole jungle theme). Sure, buying a new computer or taking friends out to eat will be quick and easy with a credit card. However, it won't be painless. If you spend $50 for dinner, plan to pay significantly more than that when the credit card interest is added to your bill. My advice: avoid credit cards the way students avoid anchovies on cafeteria pizza. Read the previous chapter for more detailed information.

Pitfall 2: Sex, Drugs, and Rock & Roll (or whatever music you like)

College is a time of exploration. For many students, that exploration includes sexual exploration. Having a dorm room or an apartment gives many students unprecedented freedom to have company whenever they please. If you and a student decide to "Netflix and chill," Mom and Dad aren't there to chaperone or ask your guest to leave when things get hot and heavy. Therefore, you have to be your own chaperone. With this newfound freedom comes a great deal of responsibility. As an adult, you have to decide if you are actually ready for this exploration. It's actually quite alright to postpone having sex until your standards of a relationship are met. You may even decide to wait until after you have graduated. The beauty of the decision is that it is yours and yours alone.

If you do decide that you want to explore, my recommendation is that you are safe. By "safe," I mean that you plan ahead by keeping protection available and getting to know your partner well. I have known several students who have had to leave college to take on the responsibility of raising a child. Others have had to make tough decisions about whether they would keep the child they have created, which could be emotionally stressful enough to derail or stall your journey to graduation. The emotional toll and financial strain of raising a child is significantly much more taxing than simply planning to be responsible about sex. Furthermore, most colleges have clinics and/or health centers that can help you plan to prevent having a child you are not ready to care for. They can also educate you on ways to stay sexually healthy. Whatever information is shared between you and your doctor or sexual health educator is strictly confidential. So, your parents won't know unless you tell them (which may not be a bad idea). No one wants you to have an infection from college that will stick with you for the rest of your life (as some do).

Sex is the not only way some college students explore. Some choose to experiment with drug use. Those drugs can be illegal substances like marijuana (depending on where you live), cocaine, LSD, or others. They can also be prescription drugs or alcohol. Regardless of the legality or chemical make-up, drugs are almost always a pitfall that college students should

The Masterpiece

avoid. They can become a financial burden, a mental block, a physical sickness, or a social disaster. In my experience, I have seen drugs send students on a tailspin of devastation.

Drugs are not a good choice for all of these previously mentioned reasons because each one is terrible. However, they also have a tendency to cause problems to layer on top of each other. For example, I once knew a student named Harry (Pitfall Harry). Harry became involved with marijuana. He started off by smoking socially at parties. Harry often told me that he never bought weed (it was always provided by friends) and that he didn't smoke a lot, implying that he had his smoking under control.

Harry's social smoking morphed into becoming a stress reliever around midterms. He liked its "medical properties," he stated. "It helps me to relax," he quipped. Later, Harry decided that weed could earn him some free smoke and a few extra dollars. He became involved in the business of marijuana. He would sell a little bit of marijuana to a select group of friends here and there, making his developing habit somewhat profitable.

When Harry's stash was found by a resident advisor, Harry ended up losing his privilege to live on campus. On top of that, he had to go to court and pay some fines. His stress reliever was turning into a very stressful experience. Harry ended up failing 2 of his classes that semester and getting "incompletes" in the other 3. When we last spoke, he was planning to make a comeback to college. Slowly, he was climbing out of this pitfall. However, weed cost him time and money that he won't get back. In addition to the time and money issue, Harry's college social life was destroyed because he had to move away from campus, his educational and social center. His relationship with his parents was also strained.

I am in no way suggesting that students can't have fun in college. In fact, I often encourage students to have a social outlet. That social outlet can include social gatherings. The key, however, is to find a balance that works for you. College can't be all work and it can't be all partying (hence the "Rock & Roll" in the heading). I have worked with students who feel that they must study 40 hours per week in order to be successful. I have also mentored students who choose to party like rock stars. Neither perspective is conducive to getting everything that your college experience has to offer. Each student must take time for self-reflection to determine the proper balance of socializing and studying. It is not a one-size-fits-all question. Your success in college will largely be determined by your custom fit efforts for your desired outcome. If that means that you study more often than your peers and socialize less, then so be it. When they say, "Turn down for what?," tell them, "my future."

Pitfall 3: Time Bank

College is different from most school experiences you'll have in life. You will have more control of your schedule than ever before. If you choose a schedule with classes on Tuesdays, Wednesdays, and Thursdays, you may have a semester with a four-day weekend. On the other hand, you may enroll in classes Monday through Friday as well as take a class online. Depending on finances, you may also have a job. Throw in a significant other or family obligations and your schedule can fill up very quickly. Time can seem very short with a variety of demands pulling you in one direction or another. If you do not manage your time, tasks can go undone. This can add to stress and cause some students to give up in the face of what seems to be an insurmountable mountain of demands. However, treating your time the way you treat your money can pay off in the long run.

When college students think about their money, they usually have limits on how they spend it. They also have security measures in place to protect their money (keeping it in a bank, having a secret pin number for ATM cards, etc.). However, their time is more accessible to the people around them. I have seen college students studying for an exam they must take the following day ditch their studying for a friend who needs a ride to the grocery store or an unexpected visitor. In these cases, the student gave up something as valuable as money: time. This is time that they will not get back and in many cases will suffer for freely spending time in a way that they would not freely spend money. The time allotted to study for the exam isn't going to magically pop up in the next 24 hours and most likely an ill-prepared student will not do as well on the exam.

Like money in the bank, students should protect their time. Set boundaries that friends and family can't infringe upon (unless there is an emergency). Communicate those boundaries to those who need to know and offer an explanation if necessary. Those who respect a student's educational priorities will understand and respect your time. Those who don't respect your time probably aren't worth your time even when you are free.

Another problem that many college students face is the habit of procrastination. Over time, some students have grown accustomed to waiting to the last minute to begin, work on, and complete assignments and other tasks. Given the fact that they only have a limited amount of time to complete tasks that may have piled up, they may not be able to develop quality work or may not complete everything on their list. Some students may even convince themselves that they don't have time to do everything. However, this is almost always not true. With proper planning, the tasks that students are assigned can be done with finesse and excellence. However, the first thing to consider about managing time is a plan. The freedom associated with going to college comes along with it a lot of factors that can consume time almost without students recognizing it. The smartphone in your pocket can eat up a few hours easily as you lie in bed or relax in your room. However, that same device can be turned into a tool to help you manage your precious time. The most important thing is that you have a plan.

Some students use planners and calendars to keep all of their tasks in order. Others use smartphones and other electronic devices to alert them of upcoming responsibilities. Still some use sticky notes strategically placed around the house to keep them informed. I recognize that everyone will come up with their own system, and as long as it keeps you organized, punctual, and effective, keep it up.

One suggestion I would make is to use a 7-day spreadsheet that details each of your waking hours. You can use this spreadsheet in two ways:

1. To assess how you have used your time in the past seven days.

2. To plan how you will use your time in the future.

Example 1 – Shelby used the chart shown here to assess how she spent the past seven days of her time. The result was that she felt like she "wasted a whole lot of time doing nothing."

The Masterpiece

Time	Sun.	Mon.	Tues.	Wed.	Thurs.	Fri.	Sat.
7:00 a.m.	Sleeping	Sleeping	Sleeping	Sleeping	Gym	Sleeping	Sleeping
8:00 a.m.			In class		In class		
9:00 a.m.							
10:00 a.m.		In class					
11:00 a.m.							Shopping
12:00 p.m.	Netflix		Lunch	At work	Lunch		
1:00 p.m.		Lunch	Studying		Studying	Lunch	
2:00 p.m.		Studying				At work	
3:00 p.m.	Lunch	Shopping	In class	FaceTime	In class		
4:00 p.m.	At work			At work			Napping
5:00 p.m.							
6:00 p.m.	FaceTime	Dinner	Dinner		Dinner		
7:00 p.m.	At work	Netflix	At work	FaceTime	At work		
8:00 p.m.				Dinner		Netflix	Party
9:00 p.m.				Netflix			
10:00 p.m.			FaceTime		Party		

After reviewing Shelby's time chart, what suggestions would you make to her?

Pitfall 4: Superhero Syndrome

When you graduate from college, you will receive a diploma to commemorate your achievement. Your name will be front and center on this document. There may be a signature or two from administrators of your institution, but your name is the most important. The graduation caps off all the hard work you put in. And yet, this accomplishment is the culmination of the efforts of a lot of people. If done efficiently, your work will be enhanced by the efforts of people who work for your institution as well as family and friends. True, you will be the one studying and turning in assignments, but there are things that professors, advisors, and loved ones should do to help. In other words, if you believe that you have to do everything and be everything to reach graduation, you may have Superhero Syndrome.

Superhero Syndrome is a phenomenon that I have seen affect many college students. They say things like, "It's my education so I have to figure it out." Or, they believe, "If I just work harder, things will get better." While I respect a student's sense of responsibility, college is a place that is designed to support the needs of students. Various offices and services exist to answer students' questions and meet their needs. Therefore, having an "I can do it all attitude" is a pitfall because it places all of the burden on the shoulders of a student, instead of the student's community. For example, students often tell me that they did not complete their FAFSA because they know they're not going to get any financial aid (in some cases this may be true, particularly if you are not a U.S. citizen or have had a disqualifying felony conviction). However, completing the

FAFSA allows a student to gain access to free money that the institution is awarding students. Your institution may use information gathered from your FAFSA to determine who they will award institutional funds like housing grants (free housing), departmental grants (money given to students based on their major), or other forms of free money. Neglecting your FAFSA can stop a stream of money that you did not know could benefit you otherwise. So, I always tell eligible students to complete the FAFSA early. There is no financial cost to apply and may lead to money that you need and didn't necessarily expect. Completing this task is one example of how activating your networks can work for your good.

Superhero Syndrome creates another pitfall because it convinces students that they do not need to ask for help. Some students believe that asking for help is a weakness. However, nothing could be further from the truth. Asking for help is actually a strength and an asset because it requires planning for the future and assessing your skills to determine what you can actually do and what you need assistance with. As a college student, some of your resources include financial advice (financial aid), course selection (academic advisor), health care (health center/clinic), academic support (tutor labs, writing center, library, etc.), and many more offices to support your quest to educational excellence. However, if you believe that you can fulfill all your needs as a student on your own, you may never be brave enough to ask for the help. That aspect of being a superhero isn't even popular in the movies considering most superheroes have a team on which to rely. In fact, the 2017 film "Justice League" had a tagline that said, "You can't save the world alone." The same is true for earning a college degree.

Pitfall 5: The Company You Keep

Most of us have heard the phrase, "Birds of a feather flock together." In the natural world, it's an observation of how birds stick with their own kind for survival. When you see geese come together in a V-formation, it's clear that they are in agreement about which direction to go. Similarly, when you see penguins waddling along together, they are typically going in the same direction. Likewise, the "birds of a feather" adage ultimately means a great deal to a college student. First, it means that you will typically head in the direction of the people you choose to keep around you. Secondly, one could conclude that those people around you will influence whether you will sink or swim.

I get it: college is not just a time for academic growth. In many cases, it is also a time to expand your social network. For many of us, the diversity found on college campuses allows us access to a variety of people from different places formerly unknown to us. There are new languages, cultures, and ethnicities represented in the people. With that diversity comes a wide variety of interests, behaviors, habits, and thoughts. For example, one of my roommates in college was born in India. In addition to English, Ajay spoke at least two other languages. During trips to the cafeteria, we ate different things and we also had different perspectives on spirituality. However, we did not allow these differences to cause friction between the two of us. Instead of discriminating against one another, we allowed two things to bring us closer: music and study. Since I was a good writer, Ajay often asked me to proofread his papers before he submitted them. In return, he would tutor me in math. Later, we found out that we both enjoyed music during study. So, I turned him on to R&B and he exposed me to some Indian instrumental music that I still enjoy today. We chose to forge a friendship that was based on our common goal of graduation.

Ajay and I both knew people who skipped class, partied too much, and studied too little. However, we only associated with them in passing. If they were birds, they were of a different feather. And when we flew, they went in another director or waddled around aimlessly looking for something to occupy their time. If invited to a party, Ajay—who was more disciplined than me—would only attend after all of his studies were done. As a result, he didn't have a whole flock of friends, just a few. Today, however, Ajay is more popular than ever. He owns a successful car dealership and manages it with the same discipline he employed in college. He can choose with whom he wishes to associate because he has a lot more free time than he did during his college days.

My time working with college students has given me a front row seat to hundreds of episodes on the social lives of college students. Some of these stories have happy endings, but many of them do not. I have seen bright, determined students arrive to college only to leave campus empty-handed because of the company they kept. Oftentimes, other pitfalls like drugs and pregnancy contributed to their departure, but rarely do students engage in reckless behavior alone. Just as there are "birds" who flock together, there are also "birds" who flop together.

Simply put, it's critical that college students select friends and associates wisely. There will be students who want to party, smoke, and drink five days a week or more. There will also be students who are practicing the discipline of time management and studying 15 hours a week or more. Regarding finding "birds," the possibilities are endless. You can find the type who fly high and work alone like eagles or mingle with the kind who scavenge for the leftovers of others like vultures. The choice is yours and having that choice is empowering. In college, you pick your friends. As a result, you also pick your future. Another old saying reads, "If you follow the crowd, you will get no further than the crowd." Your journey to your idea of success may be lonely at times, but that's OK because it is a personal journey. No one is going to work harder for your vision than you. However, there will be people who have goals similar to yours who will be eager to partner with you for a while to reach your collective goals. That goal may be an "A" on an exam or a shared business venture once the two of you graduate. Whatever you do, assess whether the people around you are pulling you up, or dragging you down.

Pitfall 6: Mental Malnutrition

Most ads and movies about college life showcase college students as beautiful, fun-loving people. The typical college scene in a film might have a shirtless young man jogging past a picturesque green landscape dotted with sunbathing coeds reading on a picnic blanket, playing an acoustic guitar, or gingerly playing hacky sack in a circle of giggling 18-year-olds. Those same young folks could easily be used for an Old Navy commercial announcing 20% off all denim. However, a real college campus will not look like this fairy tale setting. There will be people who do not look and think like you. Perhaps, your roommate will be someone you would not ordinarily associate with, causing tension in your new home. Or, maybe you have a professor who takes pride in making freshmen shed tears. Regardless of the situation, your mental health is something that you should not ignore.

Like your physical body, you should take good care of your mental health. Some would argue that taking care of your body is taking care of your mind. To some degree, this is true. For example, getting sufficient rest is good for your mind and your body. Sleep allows us to recover from illness, refresh your mind, and emotionally recover from things that bothered us the day before. Have you ever thought that something you fretted over was actually no big deal after you have had time to rest? If the answer is "yes," sleeping may have given you the clarity of mind you needed to see the situation with fresh eyes and a fresh mind.

Ignoring your mental health may leave you emotionally and mentally starved and mental starvation is not good for a college student. Managing your time (see 'Time Bank,' above) can help you with your mental health because it allows you to grant yourself time to sleep, study, and even party. Far too often, I see students neglecting the skill of time management, which leads to them mentally giving up. When they give up mentally, they know that their grades will reflect that they threw in the towel. However, once they are down, some can't seem to pull themselves up.

Here are some strategies to help college students prioritize their mental health:

Strategy	Insight
Sleep	Sleep is essential for all humans. Most health professionals suggest 7–8 hours of sleep per night. Getting rest boosts your immune system, improves memory, makes you more productive, strengthens your heart and allows you to make better decisions. Sleep is as important to a college student as it is to a newborn. Do you know how cranky they get when they don't sleep?
Drink water to stay hydrated	Your body is mostly made up of water. You need water to keep your organs, skin, eyes, and brain healthy. Starve yourself of water, and you will see and feel signs of dehydration. You won't feel your best.
Exercise	Moving your body activates your respiratory and circulatory systems. Doing so can alter the way you feel if you are feeling low. Exercise also gets you out of your room, where you can enjoy nature. The change of scenery is good for your body and mind.
Relax	You've known yourself for many years. You know what you like and what you do not enjoy. Take some time to do the things that you like to do. For some of you, that may be listening to music. For others, relaxation may be going to a museum. Remember that you are a human being and that college is a chapter in your life, so continue to do the healthy things that you enjoy as a way to take a break from studies.

Strategy	Insight
Stay connected	Keeping in touch with loved ones helps to remind you who you are and why you came to college. These people will be honest with you and should allow you to share how you feel and any challenges you are facing. If they attended college, they can share with you how they persevered.
Communicate	When you are feeling low in college, the typical reaction may be to bury your head in the sand like an ostrich. This is actually the worst thing you can do. Talk to your professors and advisors. You will find that they will offer you support. In many cases, your professors will work with you so that you earn the grade you need. The people around you are not mind readers; if you don't tell them that you need something, you probably won't get it.

College is a stressful time. For many, it will be the first time that they have ventured away from home. It may be the first time that you are responsible for your laundry, purchasing your own toiletries, and managing your own finances. You may also be surrounded by mostly strangers for the first time. Keeping in mind that everyone is feeling a sense of anxiety and nervous energy is a good thing because many times students feel like they are the only one burdened with these feelings. Like the movies and commercials, it is not popular to promote the true angst that comes along with the college transition. Therefore, you have to be able to separate fact from fiction.

Mental health challenges will be exacerbated by the college experience. If you have been diagnosed with a mental health disorder, it will be very important that you have a plan for managing your mental health. Follow your doctor's and/or mental health professional's guidance. The tips suggested above are good practice for all college students. However, they should not replace the expertise and prescriptions of your doctor.

Keep in mind that your mental health should always be a part of your routine. When times are going well, your mental health should be a priority. When things fall apart, mental health should be your priority. Keeping yourself out of the pit of mental malnutrition is preferred. However, if you fall in, stick to the plans!

The Gallery

Welcome to the Gallery

My first trip to a museum took place over thirty years ago. It was a field trip during my formative years. In fact, it was so long ago that I don't remember which one of Detroit's rich museums it was. My mind could possibly be combining several museum experiences into one, but I ask that you bear with me while I make a few points.

From memory, I remember that my museum experiences took me on a journey far and wide to places where mummies rested in ornate tombs and Egyptian hieroglyphs adorned the walls communicating in a language that I did not understand. I also remember experiences that took me through the evolution of the automobile, showing us how we got to the days of the Ford Mustang from the antiquated Model T. Finally, I recall beautiful marble floored hallways featuring framed artwork along the walls. I remember teachers shushing restless kids, urging us to take in the beauty that stood before us. But, if I'm being honest, we didn't care about Monet, Picasso, or Michaelangelo. All we knew is that we could not touch the pictures and exhibits. Some were so valuable that they were cordoned off by a red velvet rope or protected by thick panes of glass. Besides, any student knew that the true masterpiece of the entire field trip experience was the design one would make in the ketchup splattered wrapper of a cheeseburger after we impatiently waited for that familiar reward from McDonald's.

As we transition to the next chapter of this book, I want to point out some things about art and life. Then, you can read the stories of seven individuals who shared their stories about their college journey. Each story is unique, like the exhibits in a museum. Each person overcame some hardships on their way to graduation. However, each one of them experienced the satisfaction of graduating from college. Some of them graduated more than once. I believe that their stories are works of art in that they are colored by their experiences. Their individual uniqueness, while highlighted in their stories, underscores many of the similar experiences shared by all humans. Behind the diplomas there are tears, smiles, and new beginnings.

Allow me to share my observations about the following stories and how each one is a work of art:

♦ Art is subjective – You may have heard the phrase "beauty is in the eye of the beholder." This means that people each have their own ideas of what they like and don't like. I'm sure you have experienced this many times in your life. It can be something like the way you choose to wear your hair or the style of clothing you wear. It could be a preference in almost anything. The stories that follow highlight how individuals from different places can have their own interpretation of a beautiful life and move closer to that beauty through education.

♦ Art knows no bounds – You may have noticed that museums showcase art in its various forms. There are paintings, sculptures, films, musical pieces, and so much more. Similarly, creating your masterpiece through education may take form in various, even non-traditional ways. The goal should not be to duplicate exactly what someone else has done. Instead, you should consider your unique skills and natural abilities to create something new for you. Most celebrated artists have studied their craft in some way, shape, or form. However, once they understand the basics, they tend to express themselves in a way that respects the rules, yet puts their personal spin on their work.

The Masterpiece

◆ Art should "speak" to you – Vincent van Gogh painted his famous portrait "The Starry Night" in 1889. I believe one of the reasons that the painting is so well-known is the fact that many of us have witnessed stars in the sky. Along with witnessing the stars can come the emotions or feelings we experience while stargazing. Those emotions could be fun, conjuring up images of summer nights spent with friends. Conversely, the stars could remind us of a loved one who may have left us on a winter night. Either way, art should strike a chord amongst humans, resonating with us and sparking a conversation within ourselves. I believe the stories that follow will do the same. They are meant to cause you to think and have an inner dialogue with you about the future, which is ready to be molded like clay in a sculptor's hands.

◆ Art can stand the test of time – For art to be considered "classic," it should be considered a quality piece of work over many generations. Think about some styles of clothing that used to be popular, but are no longer considered beautiful. You can Google "80's fashion" or (dare I say it) "90's fashion" to prove this point. I don't believe the baggy jeans we wore in high school would be considered classic style. However, the best art can shine in any generation. It has been debated whether or not the woman painted in the Mona Lisa is classically beautiful. Some say that she is, while others say that she is average at best. What is less debatable is the value, technique, and artistry displayed in the artwork itself. We could only be so lucky that centuries from now people recall the lives that we currently live. If you live your life in a way that respects yourself and others while simultaneously fulfilling your dreams through education, that is a wonderful preface to making history.

It is my hope that you enjoy and learn from the stories in the following pages. Each individual shared with me intimate parts of their lives. For that, I am forever grateful. These are stories and lessons that are not often discussed in a public forum. The details are real, unfiltered, and precious. Take your time to take it all in. I believe it will help you in your own journey.

Tanner Bosma

"It does not do to dwell on dreams and forget to live." – Albus Dumbledore, "Sorcerer's Stone"

The Masterpiece

The distance between the city of Holland in Michigan and New York City is over 750 miles. However, when you consider other differences between the two places, they may as well be on different planets. Holland, for example, has a population of a little more than 33,000 people. New York City, on the other hand, has a population of over 8 million people. Culturally, there are differences as well. While Holland, Michigan is over 80% white, New York City is a bustling, busy, cultural mosaic wherein 57% of the people are Black, Asian, Hispanic, or other races. One could argue that the two cities couldn't be more different, but in the end the contrasts set the stage for a lively and artful story.

Tanner Bosma is an artist, specializing in painting non-objective abstract pieces, landscapes, and realistic cityscapes. Since graduating from Western Michigan University's Frostic School of Fine Arts, he is planning the next phase of his life, which includes relocating from his hometown of Holland, Michigan (where he has been teaching art) to the Big Apple. There, he plans to explore life in the cultural mecca and use his talents to leave his mark on the world. Tanner's artwork is a reflection of his thoughts, his life experiences, and his hopes for the future. Many of his pieces are abstract, which means they express emotion through colors, shapes, and textures. He also paints in the realism genre, which seeks to represent images truthfully, the way a camera would. "I want to share my love for painting and inspire others, not necessarily to paint, but even just to smile," Tanner said.

Before he decided to take on the big city, Tanner was the second born child of five to a traditional, Christian, conservative family in Holland, Michigan. His family structure, containing his father and stay-at-home mom, was considered the norm in the picturesque city on the shore of Lake Macatawa. Folks familiar with Holland, Michigan know that the town is famous for its annual Tulip Time Festival, which celebrates Holland's Dutch heritage. The most recognizable landmark in Holland, the Big Red Lighthouse, is as identifiable with the city as Lady Liberty is with New York. Legend has it that Holland is a small town with charm and big city amenities. Tanner just happens to be ready to experience the amenities of a bigger city with brighter lights.

Prior to attending Western Michigan University, Tanner enjoyed the many benefits of his small-town upbringing. Sports were a big part of the Bosma family experience. All of the children played sports, including football, basketball, and lacrosse, while Father Bosma coached basketball. Tanner refers to himself as an "odd duck," as he gravitated towards sports that focused on individual concentration and achievement such as gymnastics and diving. "While my dad was coaching, I was on the sidelines doing cartwheels and flipping, so my parents decided to support me in pursuing gymnastics," he recalls.

One of Tanner's challenges in gymnastics taught him a lesson that has served him well in life. "I remember being afraid of doing a back handspring," Tanner recalls. The thought of having to perform this maneuver was enough to cause fear in the young athlete. However, with practice and his parents' devotion to him and his sport (they had to drive him about an hour each way several times a week), the nimble gymnast squelched that fear. Ultimately, he was able to string together several back handsprings in a row, building his confidence with each bound. From that experience, Tanner learned perseverance and the importance of facing fears head on. Fortunately, this attribute would come in handy later as he navigated college and life as an artist.

The Masterpiece

As Tanner neared the end of his high school journey, he knew that he wanted to have a career in art. Yet, he was unsure how that would materialize. Being one in a graduating class of 600 highlights the size of Tanner's rather large high school. However, what he learned there caused him to gain insight into himself, his identity in the world, and what truly made him happy. Despite being born and raised in a predominately white environment, Tanner yearned for a more diverse setting. He recognized that there was more to explore about the world and himself.

During a mission trip to Palestine, Tanner narrowed down what he wanted to study in college: Art Education. "It was there that we put on a fine arts camp for Palestinian Christians," he remembers. During that trip, that took place just before Tanner's freshman year in college, all the stars aligned for him. The trip brought together dancing, sculpture, painting, photography, music and more, stoking Tanner's passion for interpreting the world through art and culture.

When it was time to look for colleges, Tanner applied to the University of Michigan (his dream school) and Western Michigan University, the school his older sister attended on a full-ride scholarship. Despite a recruiter from the University of Michigan discouraging his pursuit of studying art there, Tanner applied and was accepted. However, he ultimately decided to follow in his sister's footsteps, accepting the same scholarship that she received. This made paying for college much more manageable. Things were looking up for Tanner. He had a scholarship as well as college credits from AP classes he had taken in high school.

In college, Tanner's hunger to learn and experience his world meant that he had an eclectic group of friends and experiences.

His friends consisted of art friends, diving friends, Christian friends, and others who worked alongside him as a resident assistant. Through those friendships, he could meet his social needs and garner support in various arenas, including academics, his social life, and sports. He would need that support as he wrestled with a part of his identity that seemingly felt like a contradiction between his faith and his own being.

"I am a part of the LGBT community and that has been really hard, but college was a time for me to figure that all out," Tanner said. Once on campus, Tanner realized that his university was more accepting and comfortable with that part of his identity than his hometown. He also found that his friends were not just accepting, but they also cared about his personal well-being. Regarding his sexual identity, Tanner describes repressing that part of himself as carrying a backpack. "Every time you repress that part of you, it's like putting a stone in the backpack; when you arrive at your destination it feels like a long, arduous journey."

Tanner credits counseling in college as one of the things that helped him to grow more comfortable in his own skin. He also came to a point where he accepted that part of himself. He acknowledges that he is still evolving in this particular journey, but maintains his faith is helping him along his journey to fully living his best life.

Tanner's pieces can be viewed and purchased on his various social media sites (Tanner Bosma Art) and his art website, tannerbosma.com. His art takes the viewer on a range of journeys from abstract pieces that make you feel like a kid gazing at sky looking for images in the clouds to cityscapes and landscapes that literally take you to another place.

The Masterpiece

Tanner is also a musician, which is fitting considering many of his pieces pair well with instrumentals. Though he isn't ready to brag about his piano skills just yet, if he plays anything like he paints, then we can expect him to take the stage at Carnegie Hall while he is in New York.

When asked about things that he enjoys in his spare time, Tanner mentioned that he is a diehard Harry Potter fan. He mentioned that he has read all of the books, watched all of the movies, and even enjoyed some Harry Potter symphonies. For someone who has never enjoyed Harry Potter, it is fitting to note that Harry Potter's main themes center around confronting fears, love, fate, and acceptance. I suppose, in a way, Tanner and Harry have some things in common. The difference is that Harry uses a wand to perform his wizardry and Tanner uses a paintbrush.

Liz Burns

"Scars show us where we've been; they do not determine where we're going."

The Masterpiece

Liz Burns' story is one for the ages. Between the pages of her story, one can find tragedy, triumph, misery, and magic. Like an engaging novel, her story reels you in and keeps you hoping that the protagonist gets to enjoy a life of peace, prosperity, and love after a tumultuous beginning. Though her story has many more chapters to be written, what's there reflects some common themes of the human experience. Some of those themes include coming of age, good versus evil, metamorphosis, and the power of love.

Liz's story began on a small farm in Imlay City, Michigan, where she was the youngest of 9 siblings all named after people in the Bible. Census data from the year 2000 lists 3,597 residents of the small community, 11 of which were the Burns family. In fact, the Burns family was Liz's whole world for a time as her parents, who professed and pretended to be staunchly religious, kept their children from going to school and enjoying any activity outside of church and an occasional trip to the zoo or a baseball game. Instead, they homeschooled the Burns bunch, indoctrinating them with a mixture of religion and their own off-brand ideology. "The way I describe it is that my parents used religion as a way to isolate us, but also to justify their abuse," Liz recalls.

Though both of her parents were present, Liz remembers that her mother's spirit was not fully present during her formative years because she struggled with addiction to alcohol and medications. Her father's presence was even more sinister as he was abusive and did not want his children to develop deep meaningful relationships with one another or anyone else. "We were all abused a little bit differently," she remembers. Within her group of siblings, Liz found comfort and confusion. She recalls one of her sisters being a surrogate mother of sorts. In that sister, she found the love and care that she was denied by her actual mother. And yet, for a period of time, two other siblings and her father traumatized her by molesting her. "During that time, it was constant; at least one of them would abuse me almost every day."

Today, Liz credits the support she received from therapy and her village of supportive friends and family for helping her to move beyond the trauma. However, as a child, she was confused and experienced culture shock when at long last she made one of her many transitions. This one was the transition from being homeschooled to going to public school. Therein, Liz had to learn concepts like deadlines (which was unfamiliar) and gym class. She marveled at the idea of meeting people from other families and began to see that not all family units were like her own. Her world was starting to open up and she began to see beauty in many of the things that her parents selfishly shielded her from. Like a caterpillar in a cocoon, Liz was changing for the better.

Around the age of 10, Liz's mother decided to divorce her father, beginning another upsetting and disruptive transition in her life. Complicating things even further, Liz's mother took only her when she left her father, leaving several siblings behind to fend for themselves. Together, Liz and her mother shared an apartment. From there, she began the process of going to another school where her mother opted to put her back to the fifth grade despite Liz being a sixth grader in her previous school. The silver lining she recalls is that she went from doing poorly in her previous school to excelling in the new one.

As Liz grew, she learned she could depend on two aunts for their constant, comforting presence. "One aunt would always host a 4th of July party at her house that would start with a parade in the morning and end with fireworks that night," she fondly remembers. On Independence Day of 2008, words uttered by her sister to her aunts set in motion another whirlwind for young Liz. Her sister revealed to her aunts the horrors that they faced in their father's home. With that, one of her aunts made it her mission of getting custody of Liz and two of her siblings.

Settling into her aunt's home had its perks. Liz became an older sister of sorts to her two younger female cousins. This gave her a new perspective and a new experience in a completely different family environment, marked with movie nights and laughter. However, it wasn't all cheerful. The good times were sometimes overshadowed by court appointments and chats with social workers. "I don't really remember all of the legal stuff, but I remember them asking if I wanted my father to go to jail forever." Liz's reply to this almost unfathomable question for a child was "No," but her father was convicted of the abuse and sentenced to serve time in prison, for which he ultimately served 8 years. Also complicating things at home was the persistent abuse that came from her older brother who was also living with Liz at her aunt's home. Liz's pleas to police to investigate this abuse fell on deaf ears. The abuse stopped when her abuser turned 18 and was kicked out.

"Honestly, the next couple of years were pretty normal." Liz joined the cheer team weeks after moving in with her aunt and tried to live a peaceful existence. Her father was in prison, her abusive brother was gone, and her mother was not physically present. However, her mother began sending flowers and gifts to Liz every year on her birthday, which only reminded her of the trauma she endured under her parents' watch. Her mother ignored her aunt's attempts to stop these gifts. Near Liz's 18th birthday, her mother sent an arrangement of flowers to her school's office. From there, Liz sent a certified letter to her mother asking her to stop. There has been no contact since that letter was sent. This signified another transition in Liz's life. It marked maturity and a transition to adulthood, a new phase of life in which she decided who had access to her time and attention.

After high school, Liz enrolled in college at Western Michigan University. At that time, she was selected to receive the Seita Scholarship, which offered a significant financial award along with support from campus staff. At first, she felt apprehensive about accepting such a generous gift, but upon arriving on campus, she knew that she had found a new place to belong. Not only was this a gigantic step into her future, but it also signified a new chapter of growth and development. Though she didn't see it at the time, this campus community would change her life for the better, opening doors for her career and her personal life.

Through her Seita Scholarship, Liz would make some meaningful connections. She credits her Campus Coach, Keyla, with changing her life even before she started college. "All of the prep work she did with me helped me a great deal." A conversation with Keyla before coming to campus led to a face-to-face meeting where Keyla remembered that Liz's favorite color was blue. Keyla, whose job it was to support Liz during college, gifted her a blue bedding set. "I was like, oh my gosh, you were listening to me." Liz remembers that blue bedding made her dorm room feel like a home to her. She recalls believing that no one would listen to what she had to say, a precedent set by the police earlier in life. Though Liz had entered a new stage of life, she was keenly aware that her father had been released from prison at the same time that she transitioned to college. This added a dose of fear that would nag her as she tried to adjust to her new norm. Complicating things further, her father had tried to contact her in college and offer a financial gift. However, Liz's village wrapped its arms around her, insulating her from further attempts to reconnect.

Prior to college, Liz remembers feeling like people could see right through her. "Before college, I always felt like I didn't belong." Liz remembers people calling her a chameleon, perhaps implying that she could fit in anywhere. However, she did not consider this a compliment as she understood it to mean that people didn't have to remember her name or the value that she brought to a situation. WMU is where Liz began to feel validated and important. She credits that sense of importance to her Campus Coach and many others she met along the way. Some of that support came from an ally to the program: WMU President Dr. John Dunn. His vocal support was fortified by his presence. Annually, Dr. Dunn hosted a pool party for students in the Seita Scholars Program. These gatherings allowed Liz and other students to meet and commune with Dr. Dunn and his wife, Linda.

It was apparent that Liz was evolving after about a year in college. While she had made some tremendous strides, she began feeling a sense of loss when Dr. Dunn announced his retirement. Staff changes in the Seita Scholars Program also threatened to shake things up in her life as well. Spurred by these changes, Liz took an interest in the university's presidential search and attended a town hall meeting aimed at finding Dr. Dunn's successor. "I thought the program cares for me, so I must do this for the future students who will be served by this program."

Despite her nervous jitters, Liz stood up during the meeting and talked about the impact of the Seita Scholars Program and Dr. Dunn's leadership. She made it known that the next president needed to prioritize the program so that other students could benefit from the support. To her surprise, Liz found support from a professor attending the meeting. That professor offered her support and encouragement. "That moment confirmed that I belonged there."

The next few years would see Liz enjoying healthy relationships with friends who have become family, but also battling thoughts of dropping out of college. "There were no less than twenty times that I truly considered dropping out. What kept me going was the fact that I was telling younger students that they could graduate." Liz stayed connected to the Seita Scholars Program by working as a mentor to incoming students. This kept her busy but was not the only connection she had to the university. Somehow, Liz found time to join Phi Sigma Pi, a gender-inclusive honor fraternity. This connection led to an opportunity to work as a Student Orientation Leader, working closely with incoming freshmen. Later, Liz found the courage to run for homecoming court. "Though I didn't win, by that time, I had won in so many other ways," she remembers. It was clear that her metamorphosis was in full swing and, as graduation approached, Liz was riding higher than ever before.

The COVID-19 pandemic was a bittersweet chapter in Liz's life. The pandemic hit and impacted the last year and a half of her college journey. All of her hard work to move towards graduation was punctuated by a lackluster graduation ceremony. Due to social distancing, Liz's last semester transitioned from in-person classes to all online coursework. This meant that relationships that she had developed began to fray. Friends

The Masterpiece

of hers were moving back home or other places to finish out the semester. "I graduated via a PowerPoint sitting on my couch at home; that was very bleak to me."

Though the ending of her college career was not what she expected, Liz had a pleasant surprise developing in her life. She met her significant other, Nick. The two of them became fast friends and began making plans to share their lives together. Their dog, Phoebe, rounded out the new family that serves as Liz's family unit. The family has started their latest chapter in the metro-Detroit area. Recently, they hosted a Thanksgiving Dinner for Liz's siblings and their children. "Being their aunt is my favorite thing," she mused. During this dinner, Liz was able to host and begin connecting with them to heal from the trauma that connected and disconnected them for some time.

Liz currently works as a university recruiter for a mortgage company. Her job affords her the opportunity to visit colleges and recruit graduates into the workforce. Undoubtedly she does her work with her signature shining smile. At this time, she is poised to live her dreams for the rest of her life. Considering the fact that she is in her twenties, there are many more chapters to be written. As she grows, she will have the tunes of her favorite songs in her heart. Those include Kelly Pickler's "I Wonder" and Owl City's "Fifth of July." Both songs hold a special place in her mind. "I Wonder" reminds her of her relationship with her mother and "Fifth of July" symbolizes a new beginning. "My life truly began on the fourth of July when my aunts saved me from my previous life," she recalls.

"That was when life began for me." - Owl City, Fifth of July

Ronald Dillard, Ph.D.

The distance between Detroit and Kalamazoo is about 140 miles. Interstate 94, which runs from east to west, can take you from "the motor city" to Kalamazoo in about two hours. However, it took Ron Dillard 18 years to get there. During that 18-year interval, "Ronnie," the middle child of a single-parent home, lived in Detroit trying to figure out what the world had to offer him. "Despite Detroit's reputation of crime, drugs, and poverty, I was able to escape two of three," he recalls.

Although he grew up in a quiet, working-class neighborhood, money was somewhat scarce for the first half of Ron's life. "I can remember using food stamps to purchase food and getting Christmas packages from local charitable organizations," Ron recalls. While his family was eligible for government assistance, the home was always clean, safe, and full of love and music. In fact, young Ronald was more attracted to his mother's record player than their television and he spent more time entertaining himself by listening to music than watching TV. He would marvel at the sounds coming from the stereo speakers as the vinyl disc spun around on the platter. His hunger for music was just beginning, but it got sent into overdrive when his aunt Vivian bought him his first record: New Edition's self-titled album. "She planted a seed in my life that day," he said. From that seed, a deep love for music and creativity grew.

Detroit in the 1980s provided an interesting backdrop for growing up. Though some would have considered it a concrete jungle, where criminals ran amuck, Ron says "I did not have that experience. It was almost like I had a bubble of safety around me keeping me protected from the hazards of the big city. I honestly can't say that anything traumatic happened to me back then. However, when I look back, I see how unlikely it is that I am now a college graduate with a PhD. During my childhood, Detroit was a hotbed of drug transactions and gang violence. Fortunately for me, I was never directly affected by bullets whizzing by. The only fists that flew around me were associated with the typical spats between brothers."

Although Ron grew up in a city in crisis, he somehow managed to be absent from the scenes of crimes as they were being committed. For example, he remembers coming home from school to find that someone had burglarized the family's home and taken his sister's piggy bank, which was heavily weighted with about $300 in coins and bills. The family later found out that a hired handyman was the culprit and they never saw him or the plastic piggy again. Ron recalls, "when I arrived home, I keyed in myself and felt paralyzed with fear when I realized that I was standing in the exact spot that a burglary had occurred." Yet, the danger was gone and the only hazard was a few shards of broken glass.

"As time went on, music, family, and faith were constant forces that guided my life," Ron recalls. During his high school years, his mother unselfishly sacrificed to buy him a trumpet to play in a few high school bands. With that trumpet, Ronald was able to travel with the school's jazz band. On one occasion, the band performed at the world-famous Fox Theater in Detroit, a stage that has seen performers such as Diana Ross, Aretha Franklin, Whitney Houston, and many more. Unbeknownst to the students, there was a special guest in the audience. "As we sat on the stage adjusting our instruments and arranging our sheet music, the announcer proclaimed that Rosa Parks was in the audience," he remembers. It was at that moment that Ronald realized that education and his passion for music could take him to exciting new places and introduce him to influential people.

When it was time to apply for college, Ronald did not have the slightest idea of how to navigate the process. In addition, there was no family college fund to pay the cost to attend. "I basically applied because that's what everyone was doing, but I really did not intend to go to school," Ronald remembers. Though he applied to avoid the embarrassment, the application process was the first step in the right direction. However, when the fall arrived, Ronald quietly retreated to a job at Target to help earn his keep. That job would be one of the things that nudged him to do more than just apply to college.

A good friend, Patrick, regularly called Ronald to fill him in on all of his experiences in college. In his talks, Patrick would remind Ronald of all of the exciting things he was missing out on, including the flexible schedules, access to the recreation center, and the unlimited chicken tenders one could get in the cafeteria. With his persistence, Patrick was able to convince Ronald to trade his red shirt and khaki pants for a college sweatshirt and bookbag. "If it wasn't for Patrick, I probably would have stayed at Target," Ronald recalls.

"When I arrived on campus, it was in January, so most of the students had settled into their routines and groups," he recalls. This added an additional challenge to starting college because most every other student was not looking to make friends with "the new guy." Since money was a nagging concern, Ron took a job as Student Janitor. This allowed him to make a few bucks picking up pizza boxes around the dorm and taking out trash when the full-time custodial staff were off the clock. However, the job introduced him to many different people, some with the knowledge and power to hire him for other jobs.

"After my first year, I became a resident advisor," Ronald remembers. Resident Advisors (RA's) are students who are employed by the university to help make living in the residence halls more peaceful and enriching. One of the perks of being an RA is that your room and dining become free for you, reducing the cost of attendance by a handsome amount. You also get your own room, which makes living for free even sweeter. The training for RA's includes communication skills, conflict resolution, and creating programs to keep students engaged in activities that increase their knowledge and skills for being successful in college. It also forges relationships that will be helpful in one's future career.

The job as an RA fit Ronald's lifestyle as a student like a hand in glove. Although he didn't know it at the time, working for the university was providing him with on-the-job training for his future career in the field of Education. Choosing Secondary Education as a major, working with students was preparing him for a career that would see him doing much of the same. The reduction in cost this work afforded him didn't hurt either. "I was so busy working that I had very little time to be distracted by the pitfalls that derail so many other students."

To Ronald, college seemed to fly by. The four years it took to complete the coursework was enhanced by the jobs he worked at the university. The ease of "going to work" was as simple as rolling out of bed during much of that time. When the coursework ended, the heavy lifting began. "My first job out of college was working as a seventh-grade teacher in Detroit Public Schools," he recalls. That job came with its own challenges. He felt that the classes and internships did not fully prepare him for the reality of working in an urban, financially hemorrhaging school district. "I'm not sure that anything could have prepared me for what I saw."

Ron began teaching in Detroit Public Schools in 2002. That same year, the movie *Antwone Fisher* was released. The film left a mark on young Mr. Dillard. It provided a context for which he could examine some of the phenomena playing out in his classroom. In the film, the main character, Antwone, struggles as a recently enlisted sailor in the U.S. Navy. He is trying to escape his past which is complicated by episodes in foster care, periods of neglect, and crippling sexual abuse. "In that theater, I was able to identify themes that I had seen playing out in the lives of my students," Ron recalls. In one instance, he remembers a student using the metal encasing of a pencil eraser to cut herself. During a separate incident, a student rolled a marijuana cigarette in class, daring the teacher to challenge the tough reputation he had cultivated with the much smaller students over whom he towered. The worst news received about a student that year was that one had committed suicide. Mr. Dillard saw no warning signs in the classroom, but there was definitely something amiss in the life of the student to have him make such a tragic and irreversible decision.

The challenges of that first year of teaching were overwhelming and when the school year ended, Mr. Dillard returned to college to pursue a master's degree. "My decision was partially based on a desire to do something other than teaching, but it was also due to fear," Ron says. Ronald felt defeated and, in a way, he felt traumatized from that first year of teaching. However, his plan to flee the classroom was unsuccessful as he began teaching courses on campus as he pursued another degree. This experience showed him that it wasn't teaching and students that he feared at all. Instead, he learned that there was another way to teach and impact the lives of students who were closer to the age of Antwone Fisher in the film. There would still be challenges that students would face. Fortunately, though, Ron began to embrace helping students navigate challenges, instead of fleeing from difficulties. "I made a decision to be relentless in my support of students out of respect for the ones who may never get a chance," he remembers.

"Graduate school provided me with opportunities to reflect on my experiences in Detroit Public Schools and compare them to the experience of teaching college courses," Ron recalls. When the 18-month program was over, Mr. Dillard was prepared to jump back into teaching. When the opportunity arose, the classroom was inside of the Kalamazoo County Juvenile Home, teaching students who had been arrested and detained for various crimes. This opportunity required patience, creativity, and compassion as the students therein displayed a range of behaviors stemming from traumas, tragedies, and maltreatment. Ron learned to teach from a place of compassion without judgment. For many of the students, the school day was a break from confinement. "I always wanted to teach in a way that made them forget that they could not simply get up and leave," he recalls. The plan was to provide a platform for the students to be heard and formulate ideas that could help them challenge their previous ways of thinking that led to incarceration.

After two years of teaching at the Kalamazoo County Juvenile Home, Ron transitioned to working at his *alma mater*, Western Michigan University. This time, his role was Campus Coach. His responsibility included building relationships with students who had aged out of foster care. With those relationships, Ron could help them to gain knowledge, awareness, and skills to graduate from college. Some of the students had similar experiences growing up to his former students in Detroit and in the juvenile home. The odds were against them that they would graduate from college, but by this time, Ron had begun to specialize in helping students beat odds. He used the same formula: empathy, listening skills, no judgment, and resourcefulness.

Today, Ron, now Dr. Dillard, continues to work with students of various backgrounds. "My work supports students from all over the world from a variety of backgrounds," he proudly proclaims. While working alongside college students, Ron pursued a Ph.D. in Special Education and Sociology. He credits the resilience and inspiration of his students for his being able to complete his terminal degree. His dissertation looked at the lived experience of college graduates who are black men, born into poverty, and living with a visual impairment. "I wanted to know how individuals with so many obstacles in their path could navigate the field of education and see it to a glorious completion," he recalls. From that work, he has learned that having a supportive community and access to resources is very important. Therefore, he strives to be that and find that for his students.

As a sociologist and educator, Ron says "I now recognize several factors from my upbringing that could have derailed my admission to college and significantly limited my chances of ever getting a college degree. One of those factors was the fact that I did not have a college fund. In addition to that, I had very limited exposure to the college environment. Lastly, the culture of my environment implied that one did not necessarily need a college degree to lead a middle-class life. The folks around me seemingly lived well, took vacations, and could indulge themselves with cars and boats if they wished." They did so with jobs in auto factories and other employment that did not require a college degree.

Being one of three children to a single mother meant that basic needs were funded before other expenses. Therefore, food and shelter took a front seat to designer clothing, video games, and college funds. Indeed, Ron's mother worked wonders with her paycheck, but her philosophy about spending was to "make a dollar holler." In other words, she stressed the importance of saving and being frugal with what they had. She also taught her children the importance of hard work, which young Ronald got the opportunity to employ as a bagger at a local grocery store by age 15.

Once in high school, Ron realized that many of his peers had a leg up on college preparation. Either they had parents who had experienced college or were a part of college prep programs that gave them valuable access to local campuses, mentoring relationships, or other insight. By the time senior year rolled around, Ron recalls "I recognized just how far behind I was. As classmates started showing up with college acceptance letters and t-shirts, I nervously questioned my next move. When the fall of 1997 arrived, I stayed home while my peers packed family vans and headed off to the ivory towers of higher education."

In his personal time, Dr. Dillard continues to enjoy music. He has spent a few years working on the craft of DJing under the name D.J. Ironic. "It's ironic that it took me over thirty years to figure out that DJing was therapeutic to me," he laughs. Music was always there, but presenting a musical tapestry to an audience requires another level of creativity and caring. It is that same level and care and creativity that Dr. Dillard displays in his day job. He still listens to New Edition, with the song *Can You Stand the Rain* heavy in his rotation. The lyrics say, "On a perfect day, I know that I can count on you. When that's not possible, tell me can you weather the storm." Dr. Dillard believes that those are words to live by.

Monique Grayson

The Masterpiece

At 12 years old, Monique Grayson's curiosity was piqued during a trip to her father's hometown of San Francisco, California. This would be the first time that Monique would travel by air. The curious young girl studied every detail of the excursion, paying careful attention to the construction of the fuselage, the various buttons and levers in the cockpit, and the folks charged with defying gravity in the steel behemoth.

The plane that ignited a curiosity-turned-passion was a Boeing 757, a jet large enough to carry over 200 people. Young Monique marveled at the miracle of flight during the four-hour quest westward. However, this trip was just the beginning for the young woman who would eventually perform the same miracle over and over again as First Officer and Captain.

Later, while attending Kalamazoo Central High School, Monique took a test designed to be an assessment of her skills. With the results, students could determine a career choice that fit their unique skills and talents. When Monique's results suggested that she would thrive in a career where she could use math and science, it sealed the deal for her. Combining her interest in aviation with the skills she had honed as a student, she knew that her career was somewhere in the sky.

When it was time to decide where to go to college, Monique had two choices. She could attend the University of Minnesota, where she had been offered a scholarship to study architecture, or she could attend Western Michigan University to study aviation. After weighing her options and considering her passion, she chose to study at Western Michigan University. At the encouragement of her mother and being awarded a scholarship to Western Michigan University, the choice was clear. Her mom said, "You're going to Western," despite

Monique's desire to leave her hometown of Kalamazoo, Michigan for a warmer climate.

"So many doors opened for me at WMU," Monique fondly remembers. Although her university was in close proximity to family, Monique understood the power of expanding her network beyond those who shared her last name. Through this network she was able to meet a flight instructor who encouraged her to study abroad even though she couldn't see past the mounting challenges of becoming a pilot on American soil. Her flight instructor, Brandon Jones, was so adamant about her seeing other parts of the world that he said, "I'll pay for your trip abroad and you pay me back in your own time." Soon after, Monique took her first flight abroad. This experience encouraged her even more to focus on becoming a pilot. It was just the boost that she needed at that time to continue aiming high.

While she has many good memories from college, Monique, like all college students, had her fair share of challenges. "My challenges took a whole village to overcome," she recalls. One challenge was actually traveling to the airport to fly. "Oddly enough, I never owned a vehicle in college," she said. Like many students studying aviation at WMU, Monique had to travel 30 minutes to nearby Battle Creek, Michigan to the university's airport. Without a car, Monique had to become creative to get back and forth to the airport and the university to work towards her various certifications. "I had to sacrifice sleep sometimes to get a ride with a flight instructor who was nice enough to take me along." That sacrifice also included long hours at the airport until the flight instructor was ready to leave, or some other form of transportation became available.

In addition to the challenge of transportation, Monique faced and overcame the pitfall of insufficient funds. Later in her journey to becoming a pilot, Monique's funding became depleted. For a student training to be a pilot, this is an urgent matter as they must have funds in their account to continue footing the bills of flying. If they don't fly, their training and progress is essentially grounded. Couple the funding concern with the growing frustration that many college students develop, Monique recalls voicing her concern to her father while riding in his car.

"I remember it vividly," she recollects. "I don't know if this is something I should continue doing," she verbalized to her father. Calmly, he asked, "Is there anything else that excites you?" When Monique could think of nothing more exciting than flying, her father replied, "Finish it up." The strength of her father was the wind beneath her educational wings. It provided the encouragement she needed to continue pursuing the dream he had exposed her to a decade earlier.

Monique's financial concerns were addressed by her village of supportive people just like some of the other concerns she had. It seemed as though her family and instructors would not allow her the space to feel sorry for herself. Her village believed in her ability and would spring into action when obstacles inevitably got in her way. When faculty noticed that Ms. Grayson was lacking the funding to continue training, they took it upon themselves to come up with funding. With this gift, Monique was reenergized and more focused than ever.

Today, Monique Grayson is a First Officer with Delta Airlines. This means that she is second only to the captain of the airplane. While she does this job with grace, her story reminds us that there can be turbulence along the way. "I remember a fellow student telling me that I may as well join the circus when I shared my career goals with him," she recalls. To a person pursuing their dreams, statements like those can derail their progress if they lack confidence, academic abilities, and the support that Monique was fortunate enough to have.

As First Officer, Monique takes turns with the captain leading flights. Sometimes she has control of the plane and other times the captain does. Each flight, however, begins with paperwork, a detailed conversation with the captain and crew, and a walk around the aircraft. They discuss possible threats to safety, weather, and measures to keep everyone on the plane safe. This might include hours at the airport before and after flying, but it is part of the job.

When asked what she enjoys most about her job, Monique's reply is somewhat surprising. "I do enjoy traveling and meeting new people, but I mostly enjoy speaking to students about my journey," she said. "I also appreciate the fact that I can challenge myself every day." Aviation, it seems, is a lot like life: you have to work hard at your craft in order to soar to new heights and create a comfortable landing. This lesson was echoed during a chance encounter with one of Monique's heroes. During a visit to Tuskegee University, Monique met Colonel Charles McGee who is one of the surviving members of the Tuskegee Airmen. When they met, Colonel McGee was impressed with First Officer Grayson's accomplishments and charm. The two chatted and Monique was honored to have met such an accomplished black pilot from an era when many believe that African-Americans were not sophisticated enough to learn aviation. Not only did Colonel McGee prove the naysayers wrong, his legacy is cemented in American history while he yet lives.

The Masterpiece

In an effort to continually improve, Monique recalls learning an important lesson in an unlikely place: Dr. Suess's book "Oh, the Places You'll Go." "I had never read the book as a child and was first exposed to it when I read it to my niece," she explains. In that book, the author addresses life's uncertainties with a rhyming poem of motivation.

> *You have brains in your head.*
> *You have feet in your shoes.*
> *You can steer yourself any direction you choose.*

Another quote that motivates Monique is a quote most often credited to Henry Ford. It states, "Whether you believe you can or believe you can't, you're right." First Officer Grayson states that she uses this quote to help perfect her skills in landing a plane. For her, the feedback is sometimes instantaneous as many passengers compliment her for the safe, comfortable landing she gives them to their various destinations.

Perhaps, one of the most incredible attributes about Monique Grayson is her humility. Though she has reached a rewarding career, she recognizes that there is still much growth ahead of her professionally and personally. We are fortunate to have examples like her and lucky that she still takes time to impact the lives of others who may be interested in pursuing a career in aviation, but needing a real-life example to model their careers after.

Johnson Simon

The Masterpiece

It is no secret that Haiti produces some of the most resilient people in the world. Some would say their strength comes from the centuries-long tension with the Dominican Republic, which shares the island with Haiti. Their relationship is like conjoined twins who despise each other. Others believe that the Haitian resolve is the result of the struggles brought from poverty and hunger. Either way, it is clear that Haitians are strong, creative, and resilient.

Johnson Simon, the artist, is an example of what the human spirit can accomplish when one puts their mind to a goal. His Haitian roots appear to have embedded in him an indescribable strength while his God-given talents have grown through education and matured through life experience. Today, Johnson is an accomplished artist, beautifying canvases with his own creative brand of art. Many of his pieces capture people in action, such as the glorious ballerina that adorned the wall when I visited his art studio in Indianapolis. It was during that time that we chatted about his art, college degrees, and future plans. Every word captivated and inspired me because Johnson is a living, breathing miracle. In addition to his art, his words mesmerized me and caused me to ponder the meaning of life.

Even before birth, Johnson was a fighter. His birth is a story full of more drama and intrigue than a Netflix series. On the day of his birth, Johnson's mother went into labor and arrived at a clinic on the island of Grand Turk. The clinic was ill-equipped to handle such a complex task as his birth, so they arranged for a helicopter to take Johnson's mother to a hospital on another part of the island. During this voyage, baby Johnson's umbilical cord was wrapped around his neck, keeping precious oxygen from reaching his brain. According to doctors, Johnson was seconds away from being brain-dead when he was born. Though he survived the ordeal, the lack of oxygen resulted in Johnson developing cerebral palsy, a condition that affects body movement, coordination, and speech. Shortly after his birth, the doctors issued a damning proclamation that Johnson has defied every day since. They told his mother that he would never walk, never live independently, and never have a fully functioning brain. "But they were wrong," Johnson says with a smile.

Johnson did face challenges. Some of those challenges were connected to cerebral palsy, or "CP," but some were not. While his parents looked for a better life outside of Haiti, Johnson lived there with his grandmother. His brother, Johnnie, who was born 13 months after his birth, grew up with him there. Although CP did not have the earth-shattering impact the doctors expected, it did delay Johnson's ability to walk. This made school an impossibility for the first few years of his life since walking was how the children got to school. Day in and day out, Johnson watched as his younger brother commuted to and from school by foot, socializing with other children. "My parents would call and try to lift my spirits, but I was sad because I really wanted to go to school," he recalls.

At age five, Johnson was elated to find out that he would be moving to the United States with his parents to begin the life that they had hoped. Coming to the U.S. meant a better education and a system that could accommodate a student with his condition. "Haiti is a poor country and they did not have the resources for me." It turned out his new school in West Palm Beach, Florida was not the haven he had hoped it would be. Almost immediately, Johnson became a target for other students to pick on. "I was happy because I was able to go to school, but I got picked on because of my disability," Johnson remembers. To make matters worse, school personnel placed Johnson in special education classes because of his cerebral palsy. "They assumed that I was special ed because of my appearance, but my brain was fully functional." Ultimately, school became a source of frustration that caused Johnson depression and thoughts of suicide.

Years went by with Johnson going unchallenged in school simply because his teachers refused to believe that he could handle the academic challenges. It was not until middle school that Johnson discovered one of his natural talents. Through his mother's work as a nurse, Johnson met Michael Tischler, an older man living with multiple sclerosis. Mr. Tischler began encouraging Johnson to paint as a means to express himself. This lit a fire in Johnson, who up to this point had felt like he did not have a voice. Mr. Tischler also began to mentor Johnson and his brother Johnnie. By this time, Johnnie was also finding a passion of his own on the football field. Johnson credits Mr. Tischler for encouraging him to paint and requiring that the two brothers work on their studies and prepare for the SAT. For Johnson, it was encouraging to meet someone with a disability who was full of life. "Michael was kind of like a father to us after my parents divorced," Johnson recalls. And with Mr. Tischler in their lives, the two Simon brothers began focusing on life after secondary education.

With Johnson thriving in art and Johnnie excelling as an athlete, college recruiters began calling for Johnnie. Johnson was planning to attend art school in Boston, preparing for his first adventure in a climate with the possibility of snow. However, when Coach Cubit of Western Michigan University came to visit, he encouraged Johnson to look into their School of Art. He sweetened the deal by promising to welcome Johnson on the football field for every home game. With that, Johnson and Johnnie both moved to Kalamazoo, Michigan to begin their college journeys together. Once there, they both got their fair share of football and snow. Coach Cubit kept his promise to the Simon brothers. "I was at every home game and even spent time in the locker room," Johnson fondly remembers.

While his brother shined on the field, Johnson began making a name for himself with his paintbrushes. When he was not painting, Johnson was socializing. As a staff person at Western Michigan University, I remember seeing Johnson riding around campus in his scooter. He was always smiling and speaking to people as he passed. He stood out because of his zeal and friendly nature. His scooter was decorated with our school colors and bumper stickers that communicated his pride for his university. That personality must have gotten the attention of others at the university because Johnson became somewhat of an ambassador for WMU. He was known for his spirit. His art adorned the walls of the university president and the president's advocacy for people with disabilities will be felt for generations to come.

Johnson recognized the challenges that some people face navigating campus when they have mobility issues such as wheelchairs, scooters, and crutches. When asked what WMU could do to better understand the needs of these individuals, Johnson suggested that someone is hired to investigate these concerns. Little did he know that he would be hired to do the job! His efforts found him giving tours to students and families who had mobility concerns. If that was not enough, Johnson shed light on areas of campus that were not accessible to people in wheelchairs and scooters. As a result, there are literally places on the campus where he left his mark, such as ramps that used to be curbs or stairs.

Today, Johnson is making his mark in another state. After graduating from Western Michigan University with a bachelor's degree in fine arts, Johnson took his education a step further by enrolling in The Herron School of Art and Design at Indiana University-Purdue University Indianapolis. There, he earned a master's degree in fine arts, once again proving the doctors and skeptics wrong about his future. Johnson's art can be found hanging in the school's museum as well as his studio just a short distance away. With pride, Johnson teaches courses in painting for the same school that graduated him, bringing full circle the plan for his life.

When asked what he wants to accomplish in the future, Johnson quickly responded, "I want to give back." He states that he wants to donate money to start a scholarship in the name of his mentor, Michael Tischler, who died shortly before Johnson and Johnnie went off to college. "The Tischlers are like family to me now," he says with a chuckle. With the Michael Tischler Scholarship, Johnson would like to pay the tuition of students who, like him, thought that college was out of reach.

Johnson credits God for the blessings he has received in life. He believes that God has kept a shield of protection around him. In fact, when Johnson was scheduled to enjoy the opening of his exhibit, he found out that he was afflicted with COVID-19. Instead of enjoying the affair and greeting guests, he was in quarantine for fourteen days. His isolation ended in time for him to partake in the exhibit before it closed. And if that wasn't enough, a car hit Johnson's scooter with him in it. Though bruised, Johnson's spirit was still high and he continued to thank God for his blessings.

Johnson did not paint a vivid picture of where he wants his life to go. Instead, he seemed open to whatever doors God continues to open for him. He does want to get married and have a family, but outside of that and his will to give back to students, he seems content with the journey he is on. His paintings are vivid, lively, and often feature people moving and using their bodies to leave their mark. On his website, Johnson is quoted as having said "My art is my movement." I believe he means both literal physical movement as well as movement in mind and spirit. In our time together, he certainly moved all three of mine.

Nhung Tran-Davies

The Masterpiece

My first meeting with Dr. Nhung Tran-Davies was a dinner welcoming her to speak with students at Western Michigan University. The dinner started off like most others, with folks coming in and greeting one another, making an effort to meet our honored guest: the talented, beautiful, caring doctor, wife, mother, and advocate that is Nhung. I had no idea, however, that this dinner would take an unexpected turn, one in which we would actually need a doctor.

Feeling the good vibes that poured through the room, my daughter skipped through the room carrying a cupcake back to her seat. On the way, she disregarded the granite countertop extending from the kitchen area. She hit her head with a thud that could be heard over the lighthearted conversation. Blood began flowing, ruining the dress that she had chosen just for this occasion. There was no need to ask, "Is there a doctor in the house," because I knew for a fact that there was.

Dr. Tran-Davies kindly and patiently took my daughter to a nearby library and cared for her wound, forgoing her meal and the crowd that had gathered to welcome her. In addition to the medical care she provided my child, she sat, talked, and played with her until the tears and blood stopped. In that moment, she used the skill of a doctor, the caring of a parent, and the humility of a compassionate human being. Remarkably, she had done all this prior to fulfilling her commitment to the students she had come to inspire. I knew in that moment that we had made the right decision to bring her to our institution because she not only talked kindness and caring, but she embodied it.

Before becoming a doctor, Nhung, like all college students, had to overcome obstacles. Her specific challenges revolved around finances, relationships, and at times self-doubt. Hers is a story of amazing resilience. When it was time to address our students the following day, she humbly shared her story. Dr. Tran-Davies, who insisted on everyone calling her "Nhung," captured every heart in the room of about 200 listeners. Some shed tears; others chuckled at her wit, but all were gripped by her touching life story.

Nhung was the sixth child born to a hard-working mother in a war-torn Vietnam. During this time, food was scarce and despite the fact that her mom worked in a rice field, it was a struggle to eat even a grain of rice. Lack of food and a cruel government drove some to criminal acts. Nhung's family, however, sacrificed to ensure the survival of the smaller children. Her mother worked tirelessly to feed her children, sewing garments and traveling by wooden boat to sell whatever food products remained fresh in the hot sun. Oftentimes, there was very little to sell.

It was during these times that Nhung learned the value of hope. Her mother instilled in her children that there would be a better day coming. Fortunately, for Nhung, she was right. However, there would be dark days as well. In her speech to our students, Dr. Tran-Davies detailed what makes a person resilient. "To be resilient," she said, "a person must have Hope, Courage, Grit, and Kindness."

About forty years prior to coming to speak with our students, who, like her, have endured some remarkable challenges, Tran-Davies arrived at Edmonton International Airport in Canada. Upon her arrival, sponsors greeted her, welcomed her as an equal, and gave her a baby doll to comfort and inspire her in this new land. This gesture was recreated in recent years when Nhung, now a doctor, welcomed Syrian refugees to Canada via the same airport. Naturally, Nhung

The Masterpiece

gave the children toys when they arrived. One touching moment of her giving a girl named Alma a doll was captured on video. It was this video that led us to invite Nhung to WMU to speak with our students.

"It was hope that got us there," Dr. Tran-Davies recalled about arriving to Canada at age 5 (the same age Alma was when she arrived years later). She described the voyage from Vietnam to Malaysia in a wooden fishing boat with over 300 other individuals all filled with hope that there would be better days ahead. "I remember the nauseating, suffocating experience in the belly of the boat where people vomited, urinated, and defecated where they sat because there was little room to move." That voyage took two days and two nights and though there were still many unforeseen challenges facing these people, they were fortunate that they actually made it to land. Another boat, filled with friends and family of Nhung, never made it to any shore. Their boat didn't survive the rough waters, taking with it all the passengers and the hope that they carried with them.

The boat carrying Nhung miraculously made it to Malaysia. Once there, American tourists urged the newly arrived passengers to sink the boat to prevent the Coast Guard from dragging them back to international waters. At that time, Malaysia had been inundated with refugees and would most certainly refuse 300 more if they could. However, without a vessel, they had no choice but to take Nhung, her family, and the others in.

In the new land, Nhung's family lived in a refugee camp where they worked with their hands to build themselves a home. "To be resilient, you also have to have courage, because hope without courage is like sitting in an empty room staring out the window, all the while hoping to go outside to feel the sunshine on your face." According to Nhung, it was her mother's courage that made her get on a fishing boat with hundreds more people not knowing if the boat would hold together for the uncertain voyage. It was courage that urged Nhung's mother to agree to going to Canada after it appeared that no country would accept her and six children. And it was courage that caused a young, introverted girl who wore clothing sewn by her seamstress mother to dare to become a physician in a new country.

"From my mother's courage, I have learned that courage comes in different forms," she recalls. Courage is facing unknown dangers in the way of your dreams, but it is also daring to live those dreams. Nhung knew at a young age that she wanted to help heal sick people. Certainly, being a refugee from Vietnam, a first-generation college student whose father died in war before her birth, and a woman complicated the odds of becoming a doctor. However, Nhung refused to relent to odds. Even when she was denied admission to medical school on her first application, she didn't give up. She regrouped, studied more, and activated her courage to apply again.

In addition to dreaming of being a doctor as a teen in Canada, Nhung marveled at the connections between art and science. She fondly remembers finding beauty in even a single grain of sand. She enjoyed watching *Jurassic Park*, which fueled her desire to be both a physician and a writer, like the author of the book by the same name. Nhung's dream was realized in 2012 when she followed the lead of a friend and self-published her first children's picture book, chronicling the loving relationship between her husband (who is also a doctor) and their children.

The Masterpiece

Perhaps, one of the most admirable characteristics about Nhung is her desire to uplift others. While on her journey to graduating from medical school, Nhung traveled to Gambia in West Africa to teach children about sexual health amid an AIDS crisis. However, before going there, she returned to Vietnam to see her country of origin and roll up her sleeves to see how she could help those there. Her labor resulted in a charity to help support educational opportunities for children in Vietnam. Though the work was daunting and required the help of others, Nhung sacrificed her time to see this venture through. The end result was the Children of Vietnam Benevolent Foundation, an organization that works to improve the lives of children living in Vietnam. The organization provides resources for children to access basic needs as well as educational opportunities.

It would be impressive if Nhung's accomplishments stopped there. However, being the extraordinary person that she is, she has shown courage in her personal life. Like her own mother, Nhung is an advocate for her children. When she came to realize that new mathematics instruction was doing more harm than good to students in Alberta, Canada, she advocated for more traditional instructional methods of the past. Nhung gathered signatures and enlisted the help of parents and mathematicians to get access to more practical math practices.

According to Nhung, "hope makes us look forward to the future, courage enables us to walk through the door, and grit keeps us going once we go through the door." These are powerful words, especially when you consider the doors that Nhung has entered and the resistance that would have stopped most people. Her grit is what made her fight for other people. Her love for people seems to extend far beyond her home and her office. Her encouraging words are a beacon of light that everyone in our auditorium could see, but they do not stop there. Nhung's dream of being a writer continues to unfold as she moves ahead with more books. In fact, when Nhung left Michigan, she left me a copy of a Vietnamese cookbook that she helped create. This was a touching gesture and actually punctuated her speech and demonstrated the last component of her definition of resilience: kindness.

We can learn a lot from Nhung's life. I learned that life can be unpredictable, cruel, and complicated by circumstances beyond our control. But, I also learned that as long as we have breath in our lungs and a goal in our minds, we can accomplish great things. Indeed, education is a big factor in Nhung's journey. However, I would argue that more important than her education is her heart. I'm sure she is touching the lives of her patients, children, and community in a profound way just as she touched ours in her short visit.

I'm going to celebrate Nhung's success by making one of the dishes from her cookbook, but you can bet it will be one of the desserts. They remind me of how sweet she is!

Sruda Xedagbui

Ghanaian Proverb: You must act as if it is impossible to fail.

The Masterpiece

Ghana is one of the jewels in the crown of Africa. The country is known for its riches, which includes the land, the natural resources, and the people. While Ghana's land produces gold, oil, and a variety of produce, the people are the country's most valuable asset. From the people comes a wealth of accomplishments, spirit, and culture that goes back centuries.

This is the story of Sruda, who—like the country of Ghana—is a jewel in her own right. Her life has proven that Sruda's light is one that cannot be dimmed, despite the hardships she has overcome. Perhaps one of her superpowers is an uncanny ability to turn tragedy into triumph. Today, Sruda is a nurse working to bring patients back to health (another one of her powers). However, when I met her, she was a college student with a smile like the sun and a heart of gold. As a college advisor, it was clear to me that she was destined for greatness. I did not know at the time that part of her strength was the foundation that her family and her country had instilled in her. Yet, it was clear to me that she wasn't the typical student who was unsure of herself. Instead, she was confident and carried herself with an inexplicable pride.

While successfully balancing the demands of a college student studying nursing, Sruda also ran a small business braiding hair. In spite of her own personal challenges, she passed her classes with honors while simultaneously blessing others with hairstyles that instilled in them a sense of pride and confidence. It was as if her hands had the power to transform the essence of her clients, creating crowns of natural hair to adorn their heads. With those crowns, some of her regality was transferred to them. Her braiding also foreshadowed her ability to turn tragedy into triumph.

Sruda Xedagbui was born in the Volta Region of Ghana. She is the youngest of five girls who are the daughters of farmers. At home, her mother stressed the importance of getting a good education. Though Sruda did not know her father very well, she knows that he was a teacher. Schooling is in her blood. The community that raised her was truly Ghanaian in that folks looked out for one another, sharing food and resources so that every person would thrive. However, there were those who sought to take advantage of and exploit the kind nature, talent, and initiative of Ghanaians. On her journey, Sruda encountered people of that kind.

At the age of 12, Sruda was excited about an opportunity to come to the United States to study. Her family had been promised this opportunity through a family friend. Excitedly, they followed all of the necessary steps to make this dream come true. For some Ghanaians, an opportunity to go to school in the United States brings hope for a more prosperous future. So, Sruda trusted these so-called "sponsors" and took the opportunity.

Once she arrived in America, it became apparent to Sruda that the sponsors who lured her here to study had other things in mind. Sruda had become ensnared in the trap of human trafficking. Held in captivity, she was forced to braid hair for the purpose of enriching her captors.

From sun up to sun down, she and other young women braided hair in a salon, but earned none of the wages. It seemed, at this time, that her American Dream had instead become a nightmare. She was away from home, kept from school, and forced to labor. This was certainly not the lifestyle she had been promised and definitely not the conditions she had hoped for.

This nightmare continued until Sruda was 17 when she was rescued from this web of labor and lies. Though she had been physically held captive, her spirit to succeed remained strong. She found herself in foster care, living with a family who mainly spoke Spanish. And though this language hurdle presented another challenge, her new family treated her with a kindness and care that did not need translation. The support and freedom offered to her by her new family was enough for her to get back to her mission of getting an education.

It was decided that Sruda would not attend a traditional high school. She instead attended a school that would forgo your typical high school activities like glee club and track so that she could hit the right notes and clear the hurdles of graduation more quickly. There, she encountered teachers who believed in her ability to learn and develop her own identity and dreams of a productive future. "For a while it was odd to have people around me who complimented me," she recalls. This supportive environment was completely different from the one she had been rescued from and she took advantage by learning all she could before graduating and moving on to community college.

Unlike many of her peers in college, Sruda had not spent the years immediately prior to college taking yearbook pictures and exploring her school's social scene. She had instead worked to hone social and linguistic skills so that she could navigate this unfamiliar field of American higher education. Without question, that hard work paid off. Her strength, resolve, and past struggles were still there, but they were neatly tucked away, giving way to a beautiful smile and gentle nature. Looking back on it now, it was ingenious how Sruda used her experience working in the sinister salon and turned it into a vehicle for her own good. She used it to socialize, network, supplement her income, and beautify other students. That creativity could be a reflection of her home country, but I believe it is uniquely her.

Sruda remembers her college journey in Nursing to be a challenging one that took a lot of discipline to complete. "I did not believe in partying, just studying," she recalls. She took her opportunity very seriously. She kept her social circle limited to like-minded individuals. Instead of encouraging each other to indulge in the stereotypical college culture of bar-hopping, they spent many evenings at the library. That's where their cups runneth over.

Eventually, her hard work and sacrifice paid off. Sruda graduated, fulfilling a promise to herself and a dream of many Ghanaians. Today, she serves as a nurse doing relationship-based care with children facing challenges such as depression, suicidal thoughts, and drug use. Though her education offers a foundation from which to treat her patients, her own experiences enhance her empathy, compassion, and zeal to build up young people going through their own struggles to find their way. "God, mental health, and relationships are the most important thing to me now," she said. Fortunately, her career is allowing her to use all three. Like all nurses, Sruda has a wealth of knowledge about the human body and medicines that can be used to promote healing. However, her current role is allowing her to help her patients' minds, bodies, and souls, which at times like these is much needed.

The future looks bright for Sruda. She has plans to continue her education by becoming a nurse practitioner. In doing so, she will have more impact on the lives of patients as nurse practitioners have more authority to develop care plans for patients. This will be good for her patients as many sick people don't care what you know until they know you care.

"If you would have sat me down at age 12 and told me that I would have graduated from college and be working as a nurse in 2020, I would not have believed you," she commented. "Life is about choices and you should not let your past define who you are today."

What I have learned from Sruda is to constantly improve in all areas of life. I have also learned that all of the pieces of our lives can be used to make those improvements. My hope is that one day I can visit Ghana. I want to see the country that gave birth to such a phenomenal woman.

www.ingramcontent.com/pod-product-compliance
Lightning Source LLC
Chambersburg PA
CBHW050914160426
43194CB00011B/2397